Dr Rebecca Ray is a clinical psychologist, author and speaker. Over the course of almost two decades of practice, Rebecca (Beck) has helped hundreds of big-picture-thinking people, through courses and consultations, live a life that's fulfilling, unapologetic and free. Whilst her technique is science-backed, her approach sees her deliver both hard and heart truths and an undercurrent ethos of self-kindness first, always. Beck's unique expertise has seen her engage with thousands of people and sets her apart as one of Australia's most in-demand and authoritative voices in the personal development space.

Beck is the author of *Be Happy*, *The Universe Listens to Brave*, *The Art of Self-Kindness*, *Breakthrough* and *Setting Boundaries*. She lives in the soul-fed hills of the Sunshine Coast with the great loves of her life: her wife Nyssa, son Bennett, two rescue Irish Setters and one gangly Weimaraner.

Connect with Rebecca on her social profiles
where you'll find her under @drrebeccaray

SMALL HABITS *for a* BIG LIFE

Dr Rebecca Ray

MACMILLAN
Pan Macmillan Australia

Pan Macmillan acknowledges the Traditional Custodians of country throughout Australia and their connections to lands, waters and communities. We pay our respect to Elders past and present and extend that respect to all Aboriginal and Torres Strait Islander peoples today. We honour more than sixty thousand years of storytelling, art and culture.

Some of the people in this book have had their names changed to protect their identities.

First published 2022 in Macmillan by Pan Macmillan Australia Pty Ltd
1 Market Street, Sydney, New South Wales, Australia, 2000

NATIONAL LIBRARY OF AUSTRALIA

A catalogue record for this book is available from the National Library of Australia

Typeset in 12/18 pt Adobe Garamond Pro by Post Pre-press Group
Printed by IVE

We advise that the information contained in this book does not negate personal responsibility on the part of the reader for their own health and safety. It is recommended that individually tailored advice is sought from your healthcare or medical professional. The publishers and their respective employees, agents and authors, are not liable for injuries or damage occasioned to any person as a result of reading or following the information contained in this book.

FSC www.fsc.org MIX Paper from responsible sources FSC® C018183

The paper in this book is FSC® certified. FSC® promotes environmentally responsible, socially beneficial and economically viable management of the world's forests.

For you, dear reader, for picking up this book as a mark of willingness to shape your habits. Your commitment to your personal evolution is stunning, and I know from – personal and professional – experience that it's never easy. It's my privilege to be alongside you, no matter how many times it takes.

Contents

It's not that you've completely ignored the directives of your inner voice to, well, get your sh*t together (Wait, I need to check if your inner dialogue gets a little sweary like mine?). You've listened, and tried to make changes. Multiple times. And it turns out that changing habits is not as simple as programming yourself once to do what you know you should do, and then staying there. Humans don't operate on a set and forget basis – immediately. But the good news is that we can, when you understand the steps of habit formation. I'm here to help you take back your direction by releasing self-defeating habits and patterns of self-sabotage. I want to see you become the sole author and editor of your life: to overcome your limiting beliefs and fears and transform your self-doubt into confidence, so that you can create a life that is fulfilling, unapologetic and free. And I'm going to show you how with small steps that actually work to make a big difference.

Honesty is my love language, and I need you to know that I'm not here as someone who has discovered the secret key to having life all sorted out. As humans, we are each climbing our own mountains. From my mountain, I can see things ahead of you that you may not yet see or feel confident to navigate. I use what I know from my own climb to show you how to make your future self proud by transforming your present-moment experience.

We're going to be talking about making change for the better by editing your life to align with the things that are most important to you and finding clarity around what you want to stand for and create for yourself. To do that, we need to start with where you're at, what is working, what isn't working, and where you might be tripping yourself up or blocking yourself from moving forward.

I know you've had enough of going around in circles. There's only so many times you can *start again* before you also start to lose trust in yourself. With psychological strategies backed by the power of science, I'm going to show you how to move forward in a workable, sustainable way.

You're here because you can see a life for yourself that is meaningful, and inspiring, and full of courage, and I'm here to remind you that it's time you started living it.

You're here because the space in between where you are now and the future self you want to live into feels uncertain, and scary, and perhaps a little overwhelming, and I'm betting you don't feel quite ready (but you're willing to try anyway). Courage is always more powerful when it has company, which is why we are going to create this brave transformation together, me showing you the way, and you taking the path. Are you ready for the first small step into a bigger and better life?

1

Self-sabotage: why do we do it?

Everyone engages in some form of avoidance on a regular basis. As human beings, we are wired to reduce our discomfort as much as possible. Thousands of years ago, when we were roaming the savannah in clans, discomfort was a very real threat to survival. Feel uncertain about whether the clan approaching over the hill is friend or foe? Avoidance is the preferred option until certainty can be met. Become unwell from some berries you found on a random bush? Avoidance is the best course of action in the future. Punished by other members of the clan for failing to find water when it was needed? Avoidance of shame in the future ensures you continue to belong with your people, because that belonging is what gives you access to protection, information and resources that help you to survive.

A characteristic of a species that helps it to survive will always strengthen over time, and so today, we are great discomfort-avoiders. And a little bit of avoidance is not a problem. In fact, it can be useful when we need time out, time to replenish, or time to boost our stores of creativity and willingness to do hard things.

Self-sabotage is anything we do that gets in the way of what we need or want to be doing. It's anything we do that moves us away from being aligned with our values, even though its purpose is to assist us in avoiding discomfort in the short-term.

Avoidance becomes self-sabotage when we spend more time on self-sabotage behaviours than on doing things that are important to us, or when it moves us further away from where we want to be, or when it drains our mental, physical, emotional and spiritual energy, or time, money and resources.

Common types of self-sabotage include procrastination, making excuses for your inaction, perfectionism, listening to, and believing, negative self-talk, not taking time for self-care, comparing yourself with others, seeking approval from others, and poor time management.

HABIT TRANSFORMATION SELF-TALK EDITION	
Excuse	**Empowerment**
'I don't have time'	'I make time'
'It's too hard'	'Effort that supports my future self is worth it'
'I can't stick at anything'	'I will find the right process for me'
'I'll start on Monday'	'I'm one choice away from starting now'
'I don't have the resources/skills'	'I can seek out what I need to make this happen'
'I can't do it by myself'	'I don't have to do this alone. I can ask for help'

Self-sabotage can become a habit that may affect any area of our lives. A little Netflix is much easier than going to the gym, and before you know it, you haven't exercised in months. A busy period at work might become years of long hours that could easily lead to burnout. You tell yourself that some day, when you've got time, you'll open your own art studio. But some day is not a day of the week. The fear of failing has your inner critic screaming at you to stay safe in your comfort zone. And another decade passes, and your art studio still remains only a dream, not the reality you'd hoped to be living by now.

The elephant and the rider

Self-sabotage is not your fault. It's driven by your biology . . . and you can't help the way you're wired. The fear system in your brain responds from a place of self-protection to reduce discomfort. There are two parts of the brain that we are interested in when it comes to self-defeating habits: the left prefrontal cortex (we'll call this your smart brain) and the limbic system (we'll call this your emotional brain).

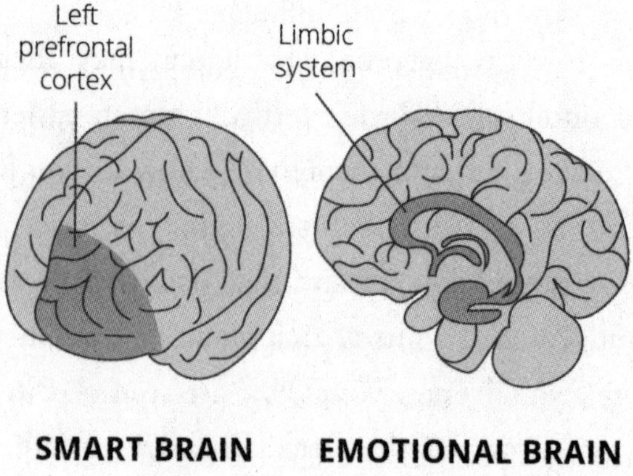

Your smart brain is the part of your brain that performs smart tasks, like logical thinking, problem-solving, decision-making and planning. It's also the part of your brain that filters your actions to ensure that they're socially appropriate. Your emotional brain is the fear centre of your brain. It controls actions for self-protection, including the survival instinct we know as the fight/flight/freeze response.

The limbic system is larger than the left prefrontal cortex, and it's fully wired in place in our brains by the time we're about 12 months old. The left prefrontal cortex is smaller and takes much longer to develop, not reaching neural pathway maturity until females are about 24 years of age and males are about 28 years of age.

Why are size and time so important when it comes to brain wiring? Because the bigger and older brain structures are, the greater their influence on our behaviour. Your emotional brain has many neural connections that have been in place since you were a baby. Your smart brain doesn't have the same level of domination over your behaviour because it's smaller and younger in comparison. Therefore, the drives of the emotional brain are harder to ignore, and it has more sway over how we act.

To make this a little easier to visualise, let's use the Buddhist metaphor of the elephant and rider, recently popularised by psychologist Jonathan Haidt. Imagine that – in terms of relative size and capacity to trigger your behaviour – your emotional brain is the large, discomfort-avoiding elephant, and your smart brain is the tiny rider sitting upon the elephant, trying to train it to behave in a way that's aligned with who you want to be.

Your elephant will take over if you don't train it to approach discomfort that's in the service of your growth rather than avoid it to stay in your safe, but unfulfilling, comfort zone. You need your rider to train your elephant to step forward. However, when your elephant takes control, self-sabotage shows up. That's when you're driven by negative thoughts and feelings, you feel disconnected from your values and your vision for your life, and you feel like change is impossible. This is when your actions happen outside of your awareness. If you've ever said to yourself that you 'just did that without realising!' after performing a self-defeating habit, this is exactly what I'm talking about. You don't have the power of choice available because your awareness is low and your elephant is on the loose.

However, when your rider is in control, you are aware of what your elephant is trying to convince you to do (or not do). Your elephant may want to run away because it seems hard or scary, but when your rider is in control, you remain focused on your values and vision for the life that you're out to create. You take action that's aligned with who you want to be. You accept discomfort in the service of living by your values and take steps to change self-defeating habits into self-supporting habits. You approach your thoughts and feelings mindfully, choosing how to respond to your thoughts and feelings rather than reacting impulsively.

The cycle of self-sabotage

First, we experience a trigger. The trigger is always some form of discomfort. It might be painful thoughts, such as,

'I can't be bothered to go to the gym. I'm too tired. I've already had such a busy day. I just don't have the energy.' Painful thoughts are accompanied by uncomfortable feelings. The feelings that accompany these thoughts about the gym might be fatigue, reluctance, overwhelm or defeat. If our awareness is low then we respond automatically, and you can probably already guess that the automatic response is avoidance. Instead of going to the gym, we think to ourselves, 'I'll go tomorrow.' And we release ourselves from the commitment and lie on the couch instead. Good old procrastination – the most common and seductive self-sabotage strategy. We don't have to push through the discomfort and, more importantly, we convince ourselves that we are absolutely committed to going to the gym tomorrow. To facing and moving through the discomfort, to doing the thing that is consistent with our values – tomorrow. And this seduction feels good. It feels like *relief*.

And in our brains, the relief is so powerful as a contrast to our discomfort at the idea of going to the gym that it stands out as important and worth repeating. Our brains reward the avoidance of discomfort by releasing a neurochemical called dopamine. Dopamine motivates us to repeat a behaviour by rewarding us with the feeling of positive satisfaction.

This is how self-sabotage becomes an unhelpful habit that we repeat unconsciously. Our brain marks the relief of avoiding discomfort with dopamine, which motivates us to continue avoiding the thing in the future. In other words, it's not you; it's your biology.

Where self-sabotage has become a habit, this relief is only temporary.

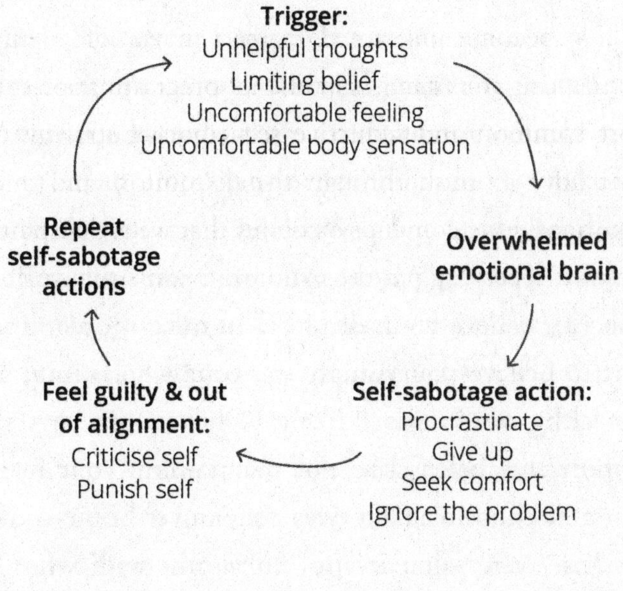

Because we don't end up going to the gym tomorrow. Or the next day. Or the day after that. Instead, we become stuck on an avoidance roundabout. This avoidance roundabout stops us from facing and moving through discomfort in order to do the hard-but-important things that fit with who we want to be and what we want to stand for. And so, we feel guilty and out of alignment and criticise or punish ourselves, which creates *more* discomfort, which then causes us to repeat our avoidance. And the cycle of self-sabotage continues.

The more we repeat an unhelpful habit, the more it can become ingrained as our sense of identity. Continuing the example of self-sabotage around health, your identity might become someone who is unfit or unhealthy. From this, you're then more likely to live into behavioural and psychological scripts that fit this identity, repeating patterns and behaviours that reaffirm who you believe yourself to be. In other words, if you start to believe that you are someone who is unfit and unhealthy, you're more likely to behave in ways that support this belief, like not maintaining your hydration and choosing take-away meals over home-cooked options, even when it's not consistent with who you really want to be.

The good news is that when we act in a way that *is* in alignment with our values, the dopamine response is even stronger. I'm going to show you how to use your biology to your advantage – to have your brain rewarding values-directed action which will then encourage you to repeat behaviour that supports you. By making a few small but consistent changes, you can transform unhelpful habits into actions towards a bigger, better life.

Take a moment

Where do you feel stuck? In what parts of your life has self-sabotage become your go-to strategy? Perhaps it's a habit that helps you avoid discomfort, but a habit that all the same is stopping you from taking action that aligns with your values. Our values represent what we want to stand for and who we want to be. Is it possible your values are being obscured by self-sabotage? When it comes to changing habits, the worst thing you can do is start with an overwhelming goal of changing too many things at once. That's a sure-fire way to set yourself up for failure. Instead, consider which *one* habit stands out to you as the one you want to change first. Starting off slow maximises your chances of success.

To identify the internal narrative that might be contributing to your self-sabotage, find a quiet place where you won't be interrupted. Give yourself time to get centred within. Ask yourself these questions and then write down whatever answers come to you intuitively. Try not to judge the process, or your answers.

1. What is holding me back right now?

   ....

   ....

   ....

2. What am I frightened of right now?

   ....

   ....

   ....

3. What is my self-sabotage trying to protect me from in this moment?

   ....

   ....

   ....

4. What story am I telling myself about this situation? Is it true?

   ....

   ....

   ....

5. Is this pattern learned from someone else?

   ....

   ....

   ....

6. What will it take to evolve this pattern beyond the cycle of keeping me stuck?

   ....

   ....

   ....

7. Who would I be without this pattern keeping me stuck?

   ....

   ....

   ....

Making these changes takes courage, grit and willingness – I'm not going to pretend it's a walk in the park! But your results will greatly depend on how you treat yourself through the process. Please go gently. Remember that you're asking yourself to face and do something hard, rather than to run away from it. Speak to yourself kindly and respectfully.

> **Going gently: Going gently is an approach of radical self-compassion that honours the role of habits of self-sabotage in your life as a protection strategy while still holding the belief in your potential to become who you desire to be.**

This doesn't mean that you give up or cop out, or that you have an excuse to be lazy, unfocused, or have no goals, or that you lack determination, or have lost your way, or that you're on the sidelines. It means choosing patience over rigid expectations; it means that you can pursue your goals without burning out; and it means that you are honest with yourself without judgement.

No transformation is simple. The neural pathways in our brains associated with unhelpful actions that have been repeated enough to become habits don't simply cease to exist because we make a decision to do things differently. Instead, it's a process of repeating new, more aligned behaviours over and over again until the fresh neural pathways take over the old neural pathways as the strongest behaviour prompts. Therefore, it's important to have realistic expectations about the process of disentangling yourself from the habits that are helping you avoid discomfort.

You'll take one step, feel a little bit of motivation and inspiration, and then the middle will get quite . . . middley. You may go sideways and even a little backwards. Remember, all forward progress is ultimately a squiggle rather than a straight line.

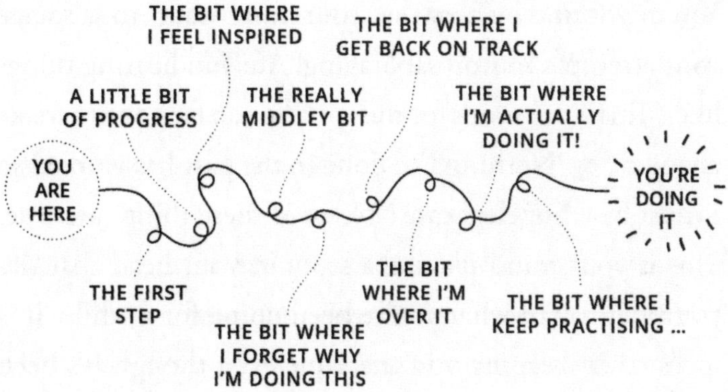

You will get off track. This is not a failure; it's your brain defaulting to the pre-existing, all-too-familiar neural pathways. Your brain is doing what it knows – it feels safer doing what it's always done. Have a little patience here, because it takes time to build new neural pathways. The research is not clear on exactly how much time it takes, because it depends on what you're changing. Part of change is that unhelpful habits will still happen, but in the coming chapters, you'll become aware as you're doing them, and you'll discover the tools and strategies that can help you do things differently.

Reckon on resistance

You might find by now that your mind wants to sabotage your attempts to stop sabotaging! Are you hearing things like, 'This won't work for me', or 'I'm too far gone to make changes', or 'Nothing I've done in the past has worked so I must be a hopeless case'? None of these things are true. This is your mind playing a story in your head that ties your identity to what you've been doing for a while. It is invested in keeping you the same even though it's been unworkable. The urge to give up on the task is actually how we give up on ourselves.

Minds don't like change (even when it's change for the better!). They remain invested in staying the same because it's easy, and easy means minimal discomfort, which is exactly what humans primarily seek. If your emotional brain is already enjoying a desirable (read: convenient) state of being, convincing it to strive for a better way of being – via a little bit of effort in the service of values alignment – won't happen without resistance. Brains will campaign heavily in support of neural pathways that help you avoid discomfort. They don't voluntarily surrender to effortful change, no matter how much you attempt to win them over by forecasting visions of you living a bigger, better life.

But that doesn't mean change is impossible. In fact, it doesn't take very much effort towards building a helpful habit before a surge of motivation will kick in.

Being aware that you're not where you want to be is part of laying foundations for new neural pathways. This is where the discomfort of change starts to be preferable to the discomfort of staying stuck. But the reality is that it gets harder before it gets easier. There may be guilt, embarrassment and/or shame when we get off track, and the pressure we put on ourselves can be a roadblock in itself. And sometimes, we're just not ready. Let me explain.

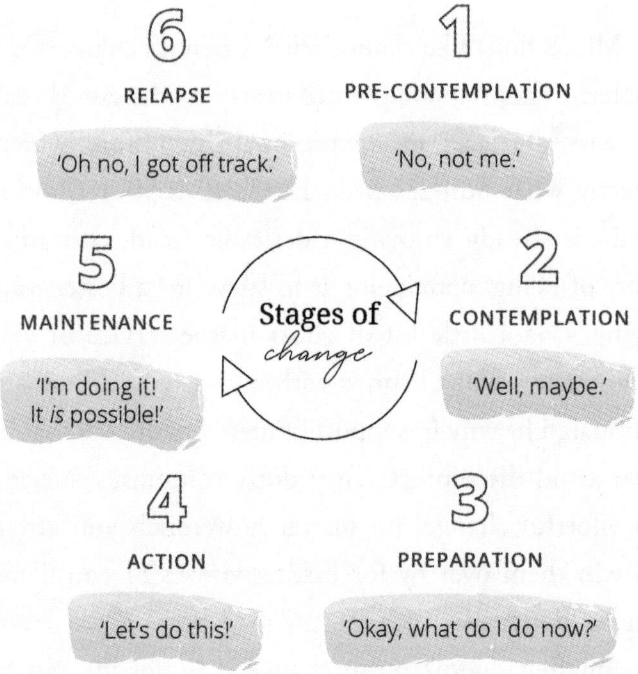

You might be well aware that you need to overhaul your habits, but that doesn't mean you'll be ready or motivated to change right now. This diagram is the Transtheoretical Model (developed by Prochaska and DiClemente in 1983), a cycle that recognises that humans find change challenging and we need to adjust our expectations to honour this. It's an exceedingly rare person that makes a change once and then sticks with it permanently!

The cycle consists of six stages:

1. **Pre-contemplation:** The stage where a problem exists, but we remain in denial about it.

   'Bad habits? Nope, I don't have any!'

2. **Contemplation:** The stage where we are approaching acknowledgement of the problem, but are not ready to do anything about it.

   'I know there are some habits that are not working for me. It's too hard to change them, though.'

3. **Preparation:** The stage where we accept there is a problem and begin research and help-seeking to address it.

   'Okay, I get it, my unhelpful habits need to be changed so I can be the person I want to be. Where do I start to learn how to do this?'

4. **Action:** The stage where we are actively making changes to remedy the problem.

'I've changed my schedule so I can fit in more time for study. And when it's time to study, I leave my phone in another room and close all my apps so that I actually do the work.'

5. **Maintenance:** The stage where the change has been embedded into our way of being.

   'Time-blocking has been a schedule-saver for me. I don't know what I did without it. My grades have improved because I make time to study now!'

6. **Relapse:** The stage where we reject the changes we are trying to make and revert to old habits and ways of being.

   'I was going along so well, and then I got COVID. Being unwell for a couple of weeks really disrupted my schedule. I just haven't gotten back into a study routine since then and I have assignment deadlines coming up that are stressful.'

Be mindful not to beat up on yourself if you notice you've been around this cycle more than a few times.

We all do. In fact, it's common to jump over or go backwards between the stages.

However, with an open mind and willing heart, change is possible, and it's possible for you.

Case study: Mira

Mira initially came to me to address her overwhelming stress levels 'because there are not enough hours in the day'. She was working from home, parenting a toddler, and carrying the majority of the household mental load while her wife worked long hours outside of the home. When I asked about her goals for therapy, she stated that therapy would feel successful for her if she could learn how to accomplish work/life balance.

We began with an exploration of Mira's patterns that were contributing to her stress. She was in a cycle of self-sabotage when it came to organising her time. She'd write an exhaustive to-do list at the beginning of the week and become overwhelmed when she perceived she was 'already behind the eight-ball' by Monday afternoon. To manage intensifying stress, Mira would procrastinate by scrolling news sites, getting lost down an online rabbit hole of 'research', or become involved in activities that were seductive because they felt productive, including cleaning, posting on social media, and redecorating her office space. This would lead her stress to further intensify because the important tasks on her to-do list remained uncompleted. Mira's self-talk would then turn critical and she would punish herself by ruminating on her looming to-do list. The flood of uncomfortable thoughts and feelings was then met with more procrastination. In the chapters to come, we'll map how Mira overcame the habit of self-sabotage to live a bigger (and more organised!) life.

2

Be clear on your why

The foundations for changing unhelpful habits into helpful ones are your reasons *why*.

Self-sabotage disconnects you from who you want to be. The disconnect exists because you are acting in a way that doesn't fit the values that are important to you. To live an expansive, inspired life, we need to take actions in line with our values, which means realigning our habits to fit the things that are most important to us.

For example, exercising and eating well are actions that support values of health and vitality. Travel to far-off places and doing things you've never done before are actions that support values of adventure and courage. Writing a book or making art or designing jewellery are actions that support values of creativity and contributing artistically to the world.

Values act as a measure of how well we are living. Not in terms of 'right' or 'wrong', but in terms of alignment with what we know is important deep down in our hearts. Our society tends to hero-worship busyness, and it's easy to get caught up in the rush of it all and forget to stop and reflect on how you are actually living. Instead, we are encouraged to measure our progress against an invisible scale of 'enoughness' that uses things like our income, dress size, number of likes on social media, whether or not we have the latest iPhone, and our capacity to look younger than our actual age as markers for a life well-lived.

But are they really?

Your values

Values are the language of our authentic self, and they are foundational in habit change because they remind us that helpful habits shape and create a life that we are proud to live, and are worth the time and effort to create.

Values act as a light in the distance, guiding us in the direction of what matters deep down in our hearts. We don't ever actually reach the light, but it's always there, helping us to find our way. They are the beacons for what we do, what we strive for, and how we interact with each other and the world at large. The simplest way to improve your wellbeing is to live congruently with your values – to make sure that you are doing what matters to you most. Sure, no one is perfect, but if you approach your life with your values at the forefront of your mind, you are likely to live more richly and meaningfully. It's about connecting with your bigger purpose. It's about having clarity around the values that are important to you. It's about not forgetting your reasons.

The language around values can be difficult to land on if you've not been exposed to it in this context before. What follows are a list of words that you might associate with values. Cast your eyes over this list and see which words resonate most for who you want to be and what you want to stand for in your life. These words then become your guiding lights.

Values words

Accepting	Authentic	Centred
Accomplishment	Autonomy	Challenged
Active	Beauty	Clear boundaries
Adventure	Brave	Committed
Affectionate	Building things	Compassionate
Ambitious	Calm	Connected
Assertive	Caring	Considerate

Consistent
Contribution
Creative
Curious
Determined
Dignified
Diplomatic
Direct
Dreamer
Drug free
Empathic
Empowered
Equality
Exciting
Financial security
Flexible
Focused
Forgiving
Free
Friendly
Fun
Generous
Goal-directed
Graceful
Grateful
Grounded
Hard working
Helpful
Honest
Independent
Indulgent
Influential
Inspired
Integrity
Kind
Leader
Learning
Leisure time
Lifestyle balance
Loving
Loyal
Mindful
Motivated
Nature
Open
Organising
Passionate
Patient
Peaceful
Persistent
Physical fitness
Planning
Positive attitude
Possessions
Prepared
Present
Proactive
Receptive
Reliable
Research
Resilient
Respect
Risk-taker
Routine
Self-disciplined
Self-respect
Self-sufficient
Sensuous
Sharing
Silly
Sincere
Spiritual
Spontaneous
Strong
Successful

Supportive	Vitality	Wisdom
Teaching	Vulnerable	
Trusting	Wellness	

David's story

David had recently discharged from the army and was re-establishing himself in the civilian workforce. He was having difficulty adjusting to life outside the military and was seeing me to address some of the coping strategies he was using that were adding to his stress rather than helping him move forward. One of those coping strategies was alcohol. David would start drinking early in the afternoon, and by the time his daughter was home from school, he was intoxicated and angry with himself, and vulnerable to projecting that anger onto his family.

I asked David to describe to me what his daughter was seeing in him as a father, and whether this was the father he wanted to be for her. His tears in response were a clear indication of how deeply painful it was for him to acknowledge that he was not being the father he wanted to be for his daughter. He was out of alignment with his values.

Realising this misalignment is not where it ends, but rather where it starts. Once we get clear on why we want to make a change, the meaning behind the change helps to motivate us to change our habits.

Take a moment

Sometimes, we can arrive at our values by working out what we don't want. Get clear around what you don't want to do. Get clear on who you don't want around you. Get clear on how you don't want to move forward. Get clear on how you don't want to feel. Following on from the gym example earlier, you might decide that you don't want to feel fatigued. Or lacking in energy. Or spending more of your time on the couch than attending to your health. Who you want to be is often deeply clarified by knowing who you don't want to be.

I don't want to do:

....

....

....

I don't want these types of people around me:

....

....

....

I don't want my future to look like:

....

....

....

I don't want to feel:

....

....

....

Your values are why you're here, opening up to the possibilities of a life where fear is transformed into freedom.

Living in sync with our values is not always easy. Sometimes, we get caught up in the struggle of being human, swamped with negative thoughts and painful feelings, and we go round in circles trying to avoid any discomfort.

This is when self-sabotage occurs. In these times, we take action based on what gives us relief rather than what is consistent with who we want to be, and these two things can often be very different. Generally, you will know when you are out of alignment with your values because your discomfort will worsen. Ignoring what's important to us leaves us feeling disconnected from our purpose and meaning. Living bravely and meaningfully is to accept that discomfort will show up. Values-directed living is often the harder path. It demands we get out of our comfort zone, do things we don't necessarily feel like doing, and trust in a little short-term pain for larger and enduring long-term gain. That is, we introduce small, helpful habits for a bigger, better life.

ACCEPTANCE *vs* **AVOIDANCE**

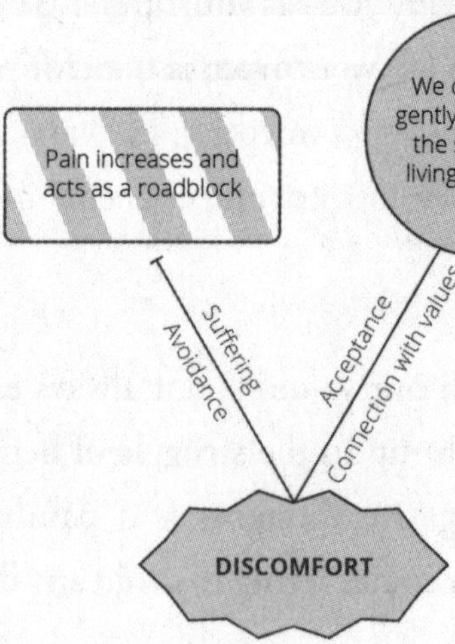

But the unconscious pull to avoid discomfort is strong – initially stronger than our desire to connect with our future self and what truly matters to us, because brains are wired for survival rather than self-actualisation. If this unconscious pull to avoid discomfort is left unchecked, then self-sabotage develops into a habit. And self-sabotage does its job of self-protection very well, which makes it hard – but not impossible – to remedy.

It's important to point out that the habit of self-sabotage is not your destiny. Once you notice yourself acting in a way that is not consistent with who you want to be, any changes you make in the service of realigning with your values are marked with significantly greater reward by your brain than any relief you may have gotten from self-sabotage. For example, going to the gym will always give you a sense of vitality that you'll never get from lying on the couch. There's no competition between the brief relief of not having to do something hard and the relative emotional weight of fulfilment and connection with what's important.

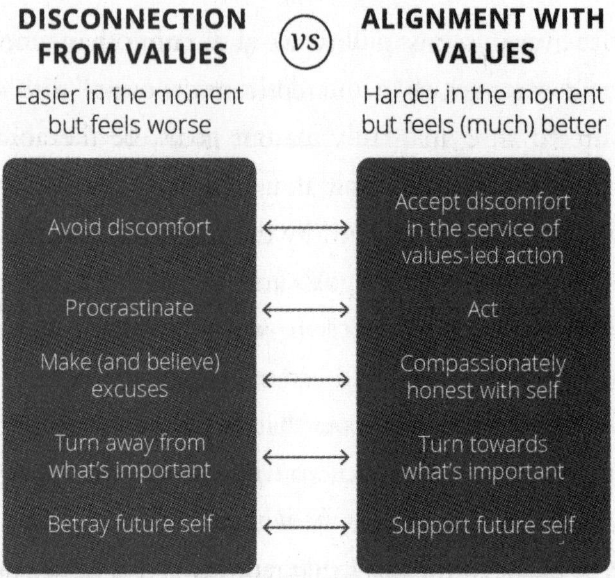
DISCONNECTION FROM VALUES
vs
ALIGNMENT WITH VALUES
Easier in the moment but feels worse
Harder in the moment but feels (much) better
Avoid discomfort
Accept discomfort in the service of values-led action
Procrastinate
Act
Make (and believe) excuses
Compassionately honest with self
Turn away from what's important
Turn towards what's important
Betray future self
Support future self

This is why getting clarity around your values is so important, because the results of living in alignment with who you want to be are second-to-none in terms of their impact on our sense of meaning, satisfaction and happiness with our lives.

Values vs Goals

An important distinction is that values are not the same as goals. The two are easily confused because Western culture, in particular, encourages us to measure the quality of our lives in terms of what we have rather than who we are and how we live. Values represent the overall direction we are heading in life, while our goals are the accomplishments we can tick off along the way. Think of your values as being represented by the sun on the horizon in the distance, while your goals are the rivers you cross, the mountains you climb, and the waypoints you pass while heading in that overall direction. Values are an ongoing process without an endpoint. Goals can be measured and completed, even if they take a while to achieve.

For example, you may have a value of being a loving partner. One of the goals that represents this value, along with many others, might be to get married. Once you're married, that goal is ticked off, while the value of being loving is ongoing and relies on consistent action to be demonstrated.

Have you ever had an experience where you have put a lot of time and effort into reaching a goal, only to successfully achieve it and notice that it didn't make you much happier? It may not have been aligned with your values. Have you failed at achieving a goal that was especially important to you and found it hard to pick yourself up again after the fall? In this case, you may have been too focused on the outcome and lost sight of your values along the way.

Sometimes we get caught up in goal achievement and become disconnected from our *why*. It's the why that will keep you going when things don't turn out as you expect them to or when they take a long time to achieve. It's the why that will help you to pursue goals that are meaningful and relevant to you in the first place. It's the why that acts as the foundation for the effort to change unhelpful habits into helpful habits that will make your future self proud.

It's important to recognise that not everyone has the same values, and there is no test to see whether your values are 'correct'. There is no right or wrong here. This is a discovery mission.

Not sure what is profoundly important to you? Look at the pain you're experiencing for the answer. Values and pain are two sides of the one coin. The pain you experience from self-sabotaging habits is an invitation to witness where you are out of alignment with who you want to be.

As we embark on this discovery journey, please be aware that this is not an invitation for your inner critic to stand on its soapbox and start berating you. Information-gathering is a critical part of awareness-building. Please also be mindful of negative self-talk. It's your mind's misguided attempts to remain stuck in what's familiar, and therefore keep you *safe*.

Nicole's story

Nicole was approaching burnout in her work as a teacher. She had given everything to her career as an early childhood educator, but she'd ignored her desire to start her own art therapy business. She was stuck in a belief that she needed to have a 'safe' job with a secure income. It had become a habit for her to stay in her comfort zone.

Her self-sabotage was showing up in the form of waiting for approval from her parents to be able to make a change and pursue what was truly meaningful for her. The approval she was waiting for wasn't going to come, because her parents wanted her to remain in education. We talked through what it would mean for her life if she continued to ignore what mattered to her in favour of pleasing her parents.

Connecting with her values led Nicole to resign, and she now runs a successful creative workshop and art therapy business which allows her to connect with the things that really matter to her.

Take a moment

Consider the area of your life where the self-defeating habit is occurring. Even if there's multiple areas of your life that are affected, choose the one that is causing you the most discomfort. Remember, we need to start slowly so as not to overwhelm your brain, which is already primed to run away, numb out or shut down when things get too difficult. Maybe it's your physical health, or your work. Perhaps it's your parenting, or your partner relationship, or your personal growth. Whichever area it's impacting upon, consider what you're avoiding in this area. What is your unhelpful habit protecting you from? Maybe it's protecting you from effort, or the impatience of slow progress, or frustration around being imperfect. Maybe it's protecting you from having to give up things you enjoy that are not all that healthy for you.

Observe your feelings. The life areas that feel unforced and satisfying, and maybe even effortless, are likely to be the areas where you are already living congruently with your values. The life areas that feel like a real struggle might be accompanied by feelings like resentment, shame or guilt. These are the areas where you're likely out of alignment with your values.

Take a couple of minutes to reflect on the following questions. You can close your eyes and consider your answers, or make your reflections even more powerful by grabbing paper and a pen and writing them down. Think about what it would look like in this area of your life if you were being your best self, living by your values and being the person you want to be in this area.

Who do you want around you?

How do you want to move forward?

How do you want to feel?

Why are you doing this?

What's most important?

What lights you up? What sparks your inspiration?

What makes you feel in flow?

What can't you stop thinking about?

What is most important to you in this area?

Who do you want to be in this area of your life?

What do you want to stand for as a person in this area?

What qualities do you want to demonstrate in this area?

How do you want to be remembered for how you show up in this area of your life?

It's these values that will help you follow through on your habit change.

Alignment

We often completely forget about our purpose and don't make the connection between the habits we're trying to create and the values that we're aligning to. Habits are more likely to stick when you attach your self-supporting behaviours to your values. For example, let's say you wanted to change your habit of eating take-away food with preparing healthy meals at home. To do this means you need to accept the discomfort that may show up around the effort required to plan meals, shop for groceries, the time to prepare food and clean up, and the conscious choice to ignore your craving for pizza and cook something healthy for you and your family.

In accepting the discomfort to develop this new, helpful habit, you get to say that you are showing up as the person you want to be: the self that values modelling to your children the importance of eating well, practising important life skills of meal planning and cooking, and nurturing your body as a vessel that is fundamental to your overall wellbeing.

While new neural pathways are developing to make your new routine automatic, the habit is difficult and takes lots of willpower. Staying close to the why behind your new habit helps you push through when it becomes difficult in the time before the behaviour is automatic.

We can't directly control our feelings (as much as we wish we could!), but we can control our actions. The awareness that you're building gives you the space to choose actions that will help you to feel the way you want to feel.

Take a moment

Now that you've identified the values that sit as the foundation of the helpful habit you want to introduce in order to live a bigger, better life, let's make this tangible. Take a moment to find a quiet space where you won't be interrupted. Use the following questions to guide you as you imagine what life will look like when you change your self-sabotaging habit to be in alignment with your values and being your best self.

The people I'm doing this for are:

....

....

....

My heart needs this because:

....

....

....

Even when I want to give up, I keep going because:

....

....

Life without alignment with these values is:

....

....

....

I'm going to start even before I'm ready because:

....

....

....

If I don't do this, it will cost me in these ways:

....

....

....

Honouring my why feels like:

....

....

....

For this new habit, I'm willing to experience self-doubt, rejection, failure and fear because:

....

....

....

For this new habit, I'm willing to face uncertainty, unfamiliar territory and no guarantees because:

....

....

....

Now that you've identified your values, how does this translate into a sure-footed direction? It doesn't. But what it *does* give you is a clear idea of what's important to your heart and soul. And it's staying close to what's important that will determine your fulfilment on your brave path.

Case study: Mira

It's easy to say that Mira simply needed to connect with her values to become more organised and stop sabotaging her time management. But her problem wasn't that she didn't know what her values were. Mira's problem was that she valued many things which competed for her time. She wanted to do everything. She wanted to connect with every value she held, every day. And as such, her to-do list became longer and her stress at there being 'not enough hours in the day' amplified. Being clear on your why is important, but it's not enough. You also need to have tools for practically following through on your why in daily life. The first of these tools that Mira and I looked at was *goals*.

3

Be SMART with your goals

Ever get a sense that time moves too quickly? All of a sudden, it's August and you still feel like it should be February. The things you were convinced you'd get around to doing last year are still sitting on a shelf in your mind rather than being present as actions in your life.

It's so easy to get caught up in our day-to-day activities that we forget to stop and look at the big picture. Goals are important because life without them can pass by unchecked all too easily. When we don't stop to reflect on whether or not we are on track to living the way we want to live, then we run the risk of living a 'some day' life, spending our time focused on the things we *plan* to do . . . some day. Months and years pass and 'some day' never arrives. The changes we want to make to improve ourselves exist only in our imagination. Have you heard the saying,

'All talk and no action'? That's what I mean here. I wonder if you've ever experienced frustration with yourself when it comes to the things you plan to do, where you talk about it but you don't ever seem to take the next step.

A common stumbling block can be waiting until your life is perfectly positioned for change. So you wait until you have the time, or the energy, or the money, or until you lose weight, or land your dream job, or until the kids start or finish school, or for a time when life is less jam-packed, rushed or demanding.

But when is that time? And how is focusing on this pretend future life affecting your experience of your life right now?

The bridge between where you currently are and where you want to be is made of goals. Goals help us to flourish. They represent something tangible that we are working towards, something that we have identified that we want to achieve. They help to prioritise and structure our time, as well as to focus our attention and increase our persistence. Goals help us to define who we are by creating a long-term vision. And of course, they give us something to look forward to!

Sounds simple enough, right? You set goals and then you give yourself the space, time and personal commitment to achieve them.

But the truth is that if it were that simple, you would have done it by now. Hold on, let me clarify: if it were that simple, you would have set goals and *achieved* them by now. I'm talking about the goals that you consider important and impactful, not goals to simply survive another week (although, in seasons when life is chaotic and difficult, a goal to make it through the day, let alone week, is perfectly reasonable). I'm not saying that your goal needs to be world-changing, or even life-changing in your own world. But I am talking about the goals that represent the life you want to live. The ones that are likely to be a little bit (or a lot) uncomfortable because they demand resources from you beyond just existing day-to-day. The goals that will make your future self high-five you with gratitude and pride.

Your goals need to be workable and achievable. There's a particular formula for framing goals that's been well-researched and practised: the SMART goal-setting method, an acronym that stands for Specific, Meaningful, Adaptive, Realistic and Time-Limited. This method will help you to set goals that are your most productive, valuable and achievable yet.

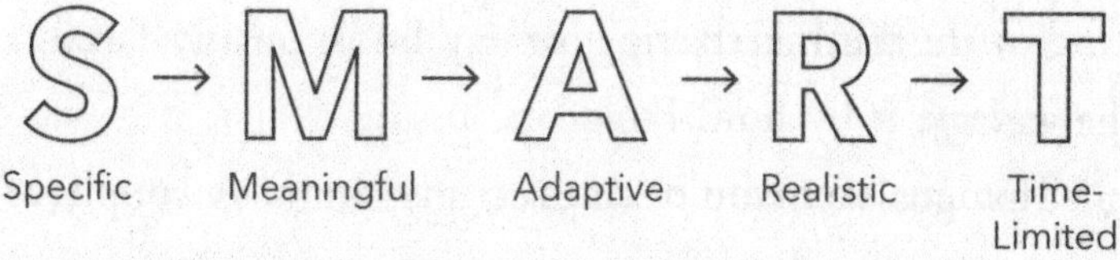

This method accounts for the fact that getting from where you are to where you want to be is usually a little more convoluted than you may first expect. Motivation is unreliable, and humans don't love sitting with discomfort, as you know, and there's not much we can do about all the other competing life demands that crop up along the way.

The SMART method

S stands for Specific. It's difficult to take action (and to know if you're succeeding) if your goals are vague. Specify the particular actions you will take, where you'll take them, who or what is involved, and how you'll measure your progress. Let's say that one of your self-sabotaging habits is to procrastinate when it comes to writing the book you've always wanted to write. An example of a vague or non-specific goal is: 'I'm going to write a book one day.' A specific goal would be: 'Every morning, I am going to sit down at my computer for 30 minutes and write the manuscript for my book on my family's genealogy.'

This goal actually belongs to my mum. A couple of years ago, she came to me to explain that she wanted to collate the years of research she's been doing on our family's genealogy into a book. My mum has not written a book before, and she was unsure of the process. The goal felt daunting to her. Achieving the goal of 'writing a book one day' was no closer a year after she first told me about it. She was putting it off because it felt big and unwieldy, and she didn't quite know how to make it happen. So, like any non-specific goal, it stayed in her head rather than landing on the page.

Slowly, I helped her to articulate the goal with specific details. What the layout of the book would look like. What would and wouldn't be included in it. How long it would be. Which software program she would write it in. And finally, how she would write it. Over time, she settled on the goal that she would spend one hour in the morning on Mondays, Wednesdays and Fridays working on her book, using Microsoft Word as her platform and dividing the book into sections based on small family groups. The specificity of this goal allowed her to translate 'writing a book one day' into concrete action that was not overwhelming, and to measure her progress by the increasing word count.

M stands for Meaningful. Set a goal that is personally meaningful to you. That means it is genuinely guided by your values (the things that represent what is important to you and what you stand for), as opposed to setting a goal just to follow rigid rules, or to please others, or to avoid some pain or discomfort. If your goals lack a sense of meaning or purpose, check in and see if they are really guided by your own values, or whether there's something within you that is adopting these goals for a reason that's outside of your authentic path. The values behind my mum's goal to write her book are that genealogy and family history are her passions and she wanted to make her work available to other family members and future generations. Record-keeping is important to her. No one else is asking her to do this. It's important to her, and that's what drives her. (I'm pleased to report that she went on to complete the book!)

A stands for Adaptive. Is the goal going to take you where you want to go? Will it help you to take your life forward in a direction that is consistent with you being your best self? Is it likely to improve the quality of your life?

My story

I once set a goal to become a pilot. My grandfather had his private pilot's licence and I loved flying with him and wondered if I could possibly fly a plane by myself one day. In terms of taking my life where I wanted to go, the context for this is that I was 18 years old. I wanted to 'do' something with my life. I wanted to do something that was outside the norm. And I wanted to be brave. This goal ticked those boxes for me, and it also allowed me to share something with my grandfather that no one else in our family shared with him. He's no longer with us, but he remains one of the great loves of my life, and I treasured our time together as I studied for my theory tests, and discussing things like the best way to land safely in a crosswind.

I achieved my private pilot's licence. It was exciting, but during the hours I'd spent flying to earn this licence, I discovered that the responsibility of flying a small piece of tin through the sky felt enormous for my anxious, approval-seeking shoulders. I'm the type of person who feels right at home when it comes to crafting words on a page or supporting someone through intense feelings.

I am not the type of person for whom numbers and visual-spatial skills come naturally. Flying was way outside of my comfort zone. I like routine and everything about flying changes daily. I like to plan my weeks and months, and while flight planning is an entire subject on its own, the act of flying is full of variety and potentially life-threatening things that could crop up at any moment. Weather. Air traffic control directives. Other traffic in the air, and so on. But rather than acknowledge that flying wasn't a good fit for me, I looked my anxiety directly in the face and decided the best way forward was to conquer it by doing more flying and turning it into a career.

While I'm a big fan of overcoming fears, what I can say about this goal is it absolutely failed to take into consideration my personality style, my non-negotiable need for routine, working within my zones of genius, and the evidence I had gathered up until that point. This evidence was clear: while I could fly well, doing more of it wasn't going to be adaptive for being my best self. In fact, what happened was I went on to get a commercial pilot's licence, a night flying rating, a multi-engine rating and an instructor's rating, and ended up extremely anxious and slightly depressed about the direction my life was taking. A direction I had created because I'd failed to acknowledge what was adaptive for me.

Your own self-knowledge is a valuable source of information for what will be adaptive for you. While conquering fears can offer a huge sense of achievement, as well as help us widen our comfort zones, you don't have to turn something that makes you very anxious into your career. Whatever your goal is, it needs to resonate with you authentically rather than be about something you do to prove a point or challenge yourself.

R in the SMART goal-setting method stands for Realistic. Make sure your goals are realistically achievable. When considering what's realistic, take into account your health, competing demands on your time, financial status, and whether you have the skills and resources to achieve it. Sometimes, it might be helpful to set smaller goals that are stepping stones to something bigger in the future.

My brother has an adventurous sense of courage. He took up stand-up paddle boarding just a few years ago. With a love for the water, and the ocean in particular, he started talking about using his newfound stand-up paddle boarding as a means to make a difference in the world. Initially, he mentioned a vague goal he described as, 'I'd like to be the first person to go some place on my stand-up paddle board. I could raise money for the feat to contribute to charity.' This goal, in its original form, is unachievable because it simply lacks the detail necessary to be able to measure and carry out. He eventually narrowed down the goal to being the first person to cross Bass Strait on a stand-up paddle board, raising money for a charity that funded education assistance for local youth.

How realistic is this, you might reasonably ask? As his older, protective sister, I asked the same thing! He was already very fit. He was an experienced ocean-goer. He'd been around the water all his life and was a strong swimmer and an accomplished sailor. He had the funds to invest in appropriate equipment and a safety team. He had the time to plan, train and devote to the feat itself. So, while this was a test of physical endurance for him and his team, it was still a realistic goal in that it was *possible*. I'm not saying your goal needs to be a world record. I'm simply saying that the resources you have for it will depend on whether it is possible and realistic. Your personality, values and the life you want for yourself will influence exactly what your goal looks like. We'll follow up on the outcome for my brother's goal in a moment.

T in SMART stands for Time-Limited. To maximise your motivation and increase the specificity of your goal, make it time-limited. Without a timeframe, it's easy to get off track and lose focus. A timeframe gives us the motivation to make 'some day' into the two weeks between 14 and 28 September. Or every Monday for six weeks. Or by 31 December. In other words, a timeframe sets a calendar container for your goal. Set a day, date and time by which you plan to achieve the goal. If you can't be that specific, set as accurate a timeframe as you can.

Take a moment

Now that you understand the SMART formula, it is time for you to apply it to the area in your life where you'd most like to replace your self-defeating habits with self-supporting habits.

Unless you're a practised goal-setter, you're likely to become overwhelmed by setting goals for every single life area at once, and therefore wind up losing motivation to work towards them.

Instead, focus on just one life area for now. It might be your health and fitness. Or it might be your relationship with yourself. Or it might be your hobbies and time for enjoyment.

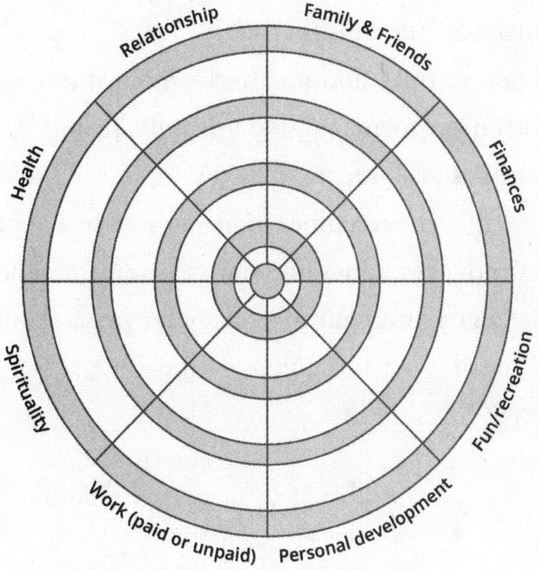

Follow the SMART formula to set a specific, meaningful, adaptive, realistic and time-limited goal in that one area of your life. Write down this goal on the worksheet that follows, or somewhere that you can return to it to look at it regularly. The act of writing down goals makes them tangible, which can increase our motivation to commit to them and follow through. Then, I encourage you to put any tendency you might have for perfectionism to the side, because the information you gather along the way will always lead to the important process of reviewing, reassessing and resetting your goal.

Setting a SMART goal and writing it down is a fantastic start. But it's only the start. Taking action towards achieving the goal gives us information about the process and ourselves that we often can't know any other way. Here are some examples of SMART goals, and the values they represent:

Life Area	**Values**	**Goal**
Health	To live an active life full of energy and vitality	To exercise 3 times per week, on Monday, Wednesday and Friday mornings, for 30 minutes
Work	To be fully present in my work life and in my home life	To draw boundaries between my work and home life by consistently leaving work at 4 pm daily and not checking my work emails until I return to work the next day

Family and friends	To be supportive and available	Text each significant person in my inner circle once per week to check in on how they are doing
Finances	Cultivating financial freedom	To budget my weekly expenses, and then spend within my means based on that budget each week
Fun/ recreation	Connecting with creativity	Engage in one creative outlet for at least 1 hour every week, beginning with a 6-week pottery course
Spirituality	Connecting with intuition	To check in with my intuition daily by journalling for 5 minutes
Relationship	To be loving, supportive and present	To arrange a date night every fortnight and consciously reduce phubbing by leaving my phone in the kitchen drawer after 6 pm until the following morning

The life area I want to transform is:

....

Now you've chosen your priority area, write down your SMART goals and the values they represent for that area. You might have goals for different timeframes within that life area, or you might just have one goal as a starting point. Remember to choose realistic goals. You can reassess at any time and build on the goals you choose.

My goals for this area are:

Short-term (next 1–4 weeks):

....

....

....

Mid-term (next 1–6 months):

....

....

....

Long-term (next 6–12 months):

....

....

....

The values that these goals represent in my life are:

1. ....
2. ....
3. ....

Reviewing your goals

Writing down your goals is a fantastic start. But it is only the start. We all know that the most important part of goal-setting is the follow through. I suggest these three steps once you have set your goals to help you achieve everything you have committed to achieving in this book and more:

1 **Review**

Look at your goals regularly. If they have a shorter timeframe, look at them daily. If they will take a little longer to achieve, read them weekly. It's important to keep your goals at the forefront of your mind to help you stay on track with your daily actions.

2 **Reassess**
Regularly reassess your progress. The goal may be too big and you've gotten stuck because you're overwhelmed or you need assistance. The goal might be too small and you've lost interest because it seems too easy. Make adjustments where necessary.

3 **Reset**
If your goals are working, great! Set more goals once you have achieved these ones. If they are not working, that's also great! Sometimes we have to discover what doesn't work to be able to set smarter goals next time. Pick up your pen and reset the goals so that they are more achievable based on your new knowledge about that goal.

When my brother first attempted crossing Bass Strait on his stand-up paddle board, he was unprepared for the weather. He experienced conflict with his boat driver because the boat driver had little understanding of the complexities of such a test of physical endurance. He didn't fully understand the impact of the cold on his body. His first attempt was a failure but a source of valuable information for his second attempt.

On his second attempt, Nick was able to find a boat captain who was more flexible in working with him and the efforts he was putting in physically, as well as changing the time of year for weather conditions that were less prohibitive. His first attempt was an education in how his body and mind responded under such conditions. While the first attempt was thwarted, it acted as a stepping stone to a second attempt, which was successful thanks to Nick's willingness to review, reassess and reset the original goal based on new information.

Let's break this down.

Reviewing your goal means looking at the goal and your progress towards it regularly. If you write your goal in a journal and never look at it again, it's a case of out of sight, out of mind. There's something about human beings and the salience of information that's kept at the forefront of thoughts. The more you remind yourself of something, the more mindful you'll be of your actions and whether or not they are consistent and aligned with your goal. If it's a goal with a shorter timeframe, look at it daily. If the goal will take a little longer to achieve, read it weekly. It's important to keep your goals front and centre to help you stay on track with your daily actions.

Reassessing your goals means you reflect on how your progress towards the result you're looking for is unfolding. If it's a habit without an end date, reassessment refers to reflecting on how aligned you are with the habitual actions you committed to. Are you doing what you said you'd do? If not, why? With compassion and curiosity, check in on where you might be stuck, where you might need help, where you've become disconnected from your vision, where you've become overwhelmed, or where you have lost interest because the bar is too low for the goal to inspire you. Make adjustments: shift the bar as necessary; seek help if needed; reconnect with your vision; research further for a different way of doing things if this method is not working.

And finally, having uncovered the sticking points in your progress and making adjustments to move forward, reset the goal in SMART goal language.

If your progress is going well, there's no need to carry out this process beyond the review step. Keep going, you're doing great! Feel free to set additional goals when you're ready.

But if you're like most of us and discover that your progress is more sideways than forwards in the beginning, then this is also great! Learning what doesn't work is just as valuable as landing upon what does.

Give yourself permission to review, reassess and reset, and then to start again.

Case study: Mira

Mira's overarching goal was to achieve work/life *balance*. While this goal is meaningful to Mira, it lacks the additional qualities of a SMART goal:

- It's not specific. What does work/life balance actually mean?
- It's not adaptive. Without defining work/life balance and learning new skills to achieve it, this goal is likely to push Mira further into self-sabotage as she chases a mirage that doesn't really exist at the end of her to-do list that she never actually reaches.
- It's not realistic. Balance implies that all things are equal. I flagged with Mira that this concept ignores the dynamic nature of the demands in our schedules and the different seasons of our lives. Seeking work/life balance is akin to striving for perfection and immediately sets Mira up to fail.

- It's not time-limited. By when is Mira supposed to have achieved the panacea of work/life balance? And what if that balance is only momentary before her time again falls into an inequitable distrubution across her values?

Goals only work if the actions that follow them are workable. Mira and I set about reconstructing her goal into something that was both practical and viable. To do that, we worked through four steps:

1. **Redefine the goal**. Instead of going for work/life balance, I introduced the concept of work/life rhythm. Work/life rhythm allows for the flexibility of changes in life seasons (e.g. the demands of a toddler versus a more independent school-aged child) and periods where work necessitates more time and focus (e.g. when approaching a deadline). In this way, the achievement of work/life 'balance' is no longer the target. Instead, it becomes how Mira honours her time as a rhythmic, ongoing process that will ebb and flow, rather than a fixed destination.

2. **Choose the values of priority right now.** Mira had been procrastinating in response to overwhelm. Her overwhelm wasn't just caused by life demands. It was also caused by her belief that it was possible to focus on all her values at once, and if she didn't, then she was missing out, not living fully and meaningfully, and/or not good enough as a person. Values are integral for guiding us to live in alignment with what's important. But like anything else, if you choose to direct your attention to one thing, you are also choosing not to direct your attention to other things. Mira struggled with this initially. She was worried that some of her values would be ignored if we chose only a handful to focus on right now. This fear soon dissipated when she checked in with herself about how her time was currently distributed between her values. The mix was considerably uneven, with work receiving most of her attention (and yet, causing her the greatest sense of overwhelm). Now convinced that choosing values to focus on *wouldn't* make things worse than they already were, Mira selected

five values that she wanted to priortise in her schedule: Being a present parent, expressing herself creatively, cultivating mental wellness, working efficiently and effectively, and carving out time to just be rather than do.

3. **Do something different to achieve a different result.** Rather than continuing to weaponise her to-do list against herself and *hope* to make time for her prioritised values, Mira learned the art of time-blocking: that is, to build her schedule on a foundation of her values rather than to make a list of tasks that are then haphazardly completed and often postponed (or shelved indefinitely). Time-blocking allowed Mira to make sure time was scheduled for her values, rather than wishing she had time leftover after her to-do list was finished for the things that were important to her. Mira time-blocked her week in advance. An example of her day is as follows, with the values each task is founded on included (as well as the daily tasks we all have to do as part of the admin of life):

Daily Planner

DATE: 15 / 02 /22

M T W T F S S

SCHEDULE		VALUE
6-7 am	Meditation	Cultivating mental wellness
7-8 am	Morning routine and daycare drop-off	Daily tasks
8-9 am	Work admin tasks	Work efficiently
9-10 am	Deep work	Work efficiently
10-11 am	Deep work	Work efficiently
11-12 pm	Deep work	Work efficiently
12-1 pm	Deep work	Work efficiently
1-2 pm	Lunch break and walk around the block	Cultivating mental wellness
2-3 pm	Painting	Creative expression
3-4 pm	Work admin and prep for tomorrow	Work efficiently
4-5 pm	Daycare pick-up and play time with son	Present parent
5-6 pm	White space	Be rather than do
6-7 pm	Dinner prep and tidy	Daily tasks
7-8 pm	White space	Be rather than do
8-9 pm	White space	Be rather than do

4. **State the goal in SMART language.** Mira's goal became, 'Spend 20 minutes every Friday afternoon planning out the following week using the time-blocking method with my prioritised values as the foundation.' This goal is repeated weekly, rather than reaching an endpoint, in the service of work/life rhythm based on her values.

5. **Review, reassess and reset.** As is the issue with most big goals, Mira's goal wasn't a case of set and forget. There were teething problems, and it took a while for her to find her groove. We'll explore the adjustments she made when reviewing her progress in the coming chapters.

4

Be ready to never feel ready

An unfortunate but seductive psychological defence is that we will, one day, feel *ready*. Ready to take action. Ready to give up unhelpful habits that are stopping us from reaching our potential, even though they are doing a great job of protecting us from perceived discomfort. Ready to start living the rest of our lives in alignment with who we truly want to be. Ready to make a change.

Why is the defence unfortunate, you ask? Because it's a myth. Feelings of perfect readiness might never come. And if they do arrive, they might not stick around for very long before they are replaced with a desire to return to avoiding discomfort and doing what's easy rather than what requires effort but is worth it, in the long run.

We convince ourselves that we'll start one day, or some day, or Monday, or the first day of the month, or 1 January, or when all the stress of life has disappeared, or when we have the money, and the time, and the energy, and the motivation, or when person X gives us their approval. The problem with this mindset is that it's placing your future in the hands of someone else and/or your internal experiences that are not within your full control; that is, your thoughts and your feelings.

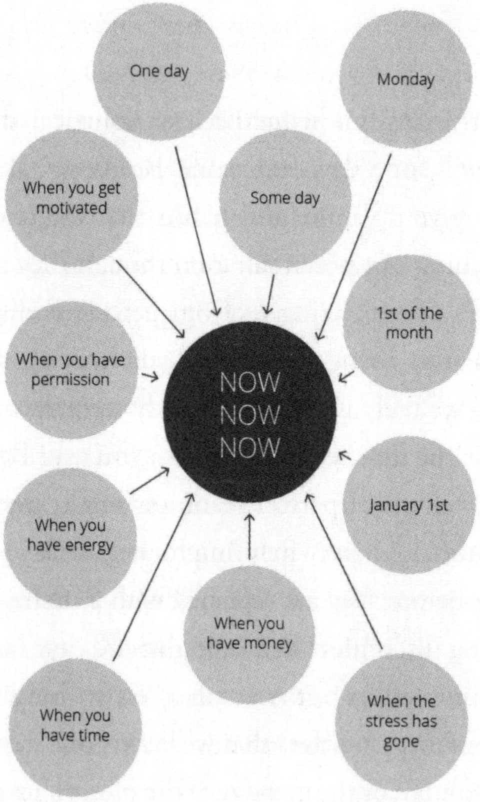

The myth of feeling ready

You wait to feel ready. And wait. And wait . . .

Feelings are fickle. You wait for your mind to get on board with the future you're trying to create. But thoughts are unreliable and minds like to focus on the negative to ensure we keep surviving.

Sometimes, waiting to be ready can be helpful. Some people reach a date that is meaningful and marks a new beginning for them. New Year's Day, or Monday, or a birthday, or another important anniversary can be a deciding date that leads some people to draw a line between an old way of being and the transition into a new way of being. But for others, dates like this can lead to high expectations, a big jump out of the gate, and then a quick U-turn towards the old ways of being because change is uncomfortable, motivation vacillates, and initial expectations might have been unrealistic. In other words, the pressure to be perfect from this date onwards is often overwhelming for our brains.

So, will waiting for a particular date to start be helpful for *you*? It depends. It depends on how many times you've tried to change your self-sabotaging habits previously; on whether or not you've hit rock bottom yet; on the level of support you have around you; on how well-planned the new habit is; on how meaningful the desired change is to you; and on how skilled you are at being able to sit with discomfort while holding on to the values behind the change you want to make.

These things don't necessarily mean that you'll feel entirely ready or comfortable with the change on which you're about to embark just because the calendar changes. Or because you're trying for the first or the fifth time. Or because you feel like you've hit rock bottom and you're sick of being the way you've been. Or because you've done a lot of personal growth work and understand how to sit with discomfort.

Getting comfortable with discomfort

You're probably getting the picture now that readiness is not really a *thing* when it comes to letting go of patterns that help us to avoid discomfort. Because as much as these self-defeating habits hold us back, they also feel protective, safe and necessary. Rewiring our brains to be able to create and maintain new, aligned habits means also facing discomfort willingly, and learning that there are other, healthier ways that we can meet our needs.

During that learning process, brains are usually very reluctant to participate in change. They like to follow the neural pathways they already know, to continue doing what they have been doing. This is especially true when the self-defeating habits appear to *work*, at least by your brain's definition of what works. Your brain has a series of checkboxes to note if a habit works and is therefore worth repeating:

1. Does it take away short-term discomfort? Check.
2. Is it easy in terms of time and effort? Check.
3. Does it bring pleasant feelings in the moment or, even better, reduce unpleasant feelings in the moment? Check.
4. Does it meet an otherwise unmet need? Check.

Once a habit checks these boxes, your brain will lobby pretty darn hard to keep that habit in the loop of automatic behaviours, even when repeating the behaviour is pushing you further away from where you want to be in life. Even when the behaviour is not consistent with how you see your future self. That outcome doesn't matter so much to your brain, which prioritises short-term satisfaction and/or relief above anything else.

Your best future self, though, is relying on you to connect with long-term satisfaction. It is relying on you to be able to delay immediate gratification, to be able to accept discomfort in the present moment, and to be able to do hard things in the service of living a life oriented around your values – the ones that represent your highest potential. Because the secret is that nothing feels quite as fulfilling as living aligned with your best self.

But this is why readiness is so difficult to arrive at. It's challenging to feel ready to let go of the things that make life a little easier right now in order to commit to making life better in the long run. I'm not saying it's impossible – we both know that it's absolutely possible. For some time, you've been watching others achieve the things you desperately want in your own life, and that brings feelings of frustration, helplessness and even hopelessness.

Motivation

Habit change is definitely possible, but it requires you to nurture yourself, and your brain, through a period of change from unconscious and automatic habit repetition, to activating your sense of inner leadership. In leading yourself more effectively, you can then identify your needs, meet them in a healthy way, and commit to your future self through the creation of new habits that are in alignment with who you want to be.

So, if a sense of readiness is not what you need, then maybe motivation is the key, right? Um . . . no.

I also wish it were that easy, and that stores of motivation sat in tablet form in jars on shelves in a supermarket right down the road from you, available for purchase any time you need a little boost to light the fire in your belly.

But, like all the other feelings we experience, motivation can't be turned on and off like a power switch. And to complicate things further, not all motivation is made the same, and different types of motivation lead to different results.

There are three different types of motivation: external motivation, goal-based motivation, and process or journey-based motivation.

External motivation is motivation that you experience to avoid a negative outcome or consequence coming from some kind of force outside yourself.

Aisha's story

I had a client who worked in a call centre. Aisha's job was to make as many cold calls to potential customers as possible per hour. She had to repeat the same script over and over again in the hopes of landing on someone who would buy the product that the company sold. Toilet breaks were timed, and if employees didn't make enough sales each week, they were punished with marks against their name on a whiteboard in front of the entire team. Aisha continued in this role only because she was motivated to pay her bills, thus avoiding the consequence of having her rent in arrears or her power cut off. She worked hard in the role to avoid being shamed in front of her teammates, not because she found the work fulfilling or rewarding. Aisha didn't enjoy her job. She felt that her work wasn't meaningful, and she found the conditions stressful. Aisha wasn't in a position to leave her job until she found alternative employment. To help her cope in the meantime, we reframed how she viewed her work. Rather than just a means to pay her bills, Aisha practised offering gratitude to herself for her tenacity to stay in a difficult job while searching for more fulfilling work. She also focused on connecting with customers during phone calls by asking them how their day was going and making pleasant small talk where possible. These small adjustments didn't change the fact that the organisational culture in which Aisha worked was cold and exploitative. But they did allow Aisha to focus more resiliently until she could find a new position elsewhere.

Goal-based motivation is motivation that we follow that is tied only to an outcome.

It doesn't take into account the blood, sweat and tears to achieve the goal. Instead, it is tied only to the completion of the goal itself. But what happens with this kind of motivation is as soon as the goal is achieved, the motivation disappears, unless it's then shifted to the outcome of a new goal. It's not motivation that is sustainable and it can often lead to burnout in people who are pursuing goals that can take a long time to achieve, for example losing weight or completing university studies.

Process-based motivation is motivation that is fuelled by the journey itself.

It means that we focus on the process, the daily efforts towards something meaningful, the satisfaction of overcoming small problems and challenges as they occur along the way, and the little wins that bring us closer to a larger goal. This is the kind of motivation that is about daily action in line with values. It's process-based motivation that helps us to interrupt the patterns of self-sabotage and be able to change existing habits into new habits that help us to be our best selves.

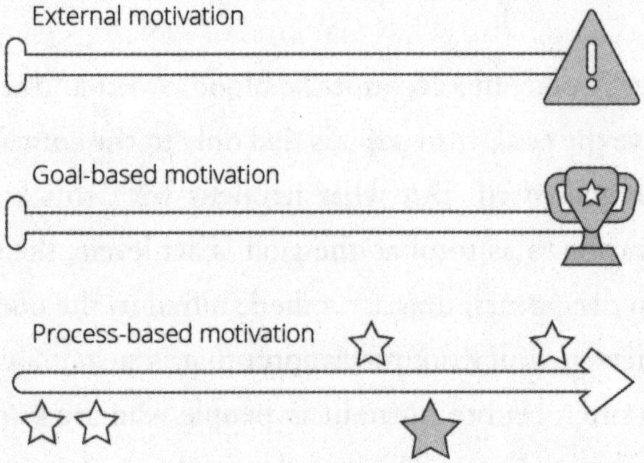

Process-based motivation is the type of motivation that allows you to focus on the journey, even when you're not quite where you want to be yet.

It's the motivation that recognises that you're on a path that fits for you, no matter how long that path is, until you conquer the next mountain of accomplishment.

The reality is that motivation is fickle. And even while process-based motivation is the most useful for developing new habits, it's not perfect, and feeling any kind of motivation is never guaranteed, because feelings themselves are always transient. So, if we rely on motivation to show up before we take action, we could be waiting a long while, and who has that kind of time to waste when trying to live a bigger, better life?

If you're asking, 'How do I take action when I don't feel ready *and* I don't feel like it?' then well done, because this is the million-dollar question. Thankfully, you don't need a million dollars to solve it – but it does help to understand control. It's important to understand that the desire for control is seductive because, as humans, we feel safer by convincing ourselves that we have control over things that we don't have much control over at all. The best way to manage it is to use it to your advantage.

By understanding what you can and can't control, you can make a conscious choice on where you choose to spend your energy to get the most out of your days, weeks, months and years.

The things we can't control include: our thoughts, feelings, body sensations, sometimes our circumstances, the past, and other people. So, if you're spending your time and energy on these things, it's not the most effective use of your personal resources. The things we can control are our attention and, most importantly, our actions.

You can't control your motivation or sense of readiness because they are both feelings. You *can* control what you do – even when your feelings don't show up in the ways that you wish they would to make your change process easier!

We can control our actions. Even when our thoughts and feelings are not on board. You can get up at 5 am, get dressed in your activewear, put your runners on, and go for a walk, even when you feel tired, and your mind is telling you that, 'It's too cold' and 'Too hard' and 'I'll do it tomorrow'.

I'm going to let you in on a little secret. It's the choices we make in how to respond to our thoughts and feelings that shape our lives, and bring our actions into alignment with the person we want to be.

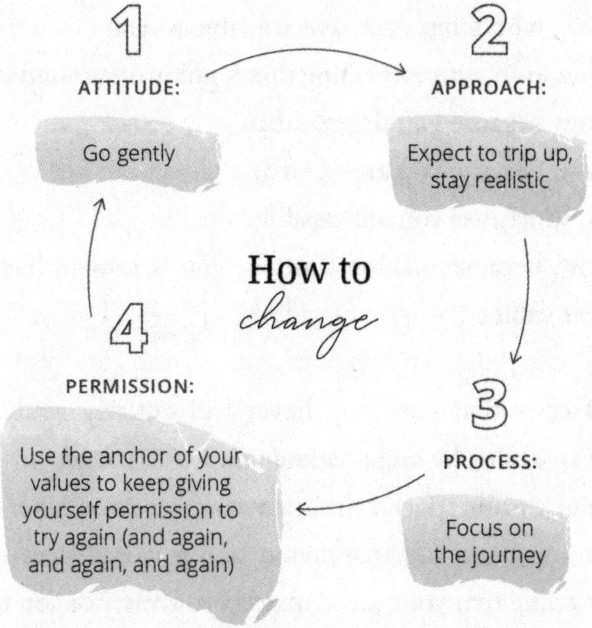
1
ATTITUDE:
Go gently
2
APPROACH:
Expect to trip up, stay realistic
How to change
3
PROCESS:
Focus on the journey
4
PERMISSION:
Use the anchor of your values to keep giving yourself permission to try again (and again, and again, and again)

Give yourself permission to start *now*. To give it a go. To test it out. This is a chance to get clarity on what does and doesn't work for you. It's a chance to start building evidence in your brain that change is possible. And, paradoxically, the boost you'll get from taking action in line with the life you're out to create is second-to-none when it comes to creating more motivation!

To do this though, you might need to challenge your mindset slightly. Get curious about the process and what shows up for you when I encourage you to consider starting. The time to start is:

Now, with what you have available to you.
Now, even with everything that is going on around you.
Now, because you deserve this.
Now, because you are worthy.
Now, because you are capable.
Now, because making time for you is how to live by your values.

The fact is that you may never feel entirely ready or motivated. But by taking action, you create momentum, and momentum triggers the brain to release dopamine, and dopamine marks a new behaviour as one worth repeating.

Be aware that your mind may try to convince you that you'll just engage in your old, self-sabotaging habit 'one last time'. One last meal before your diet kicks in. One last year in the job that you dislike. One more online purchase before you start saving for your dream trip overseas. Except it's rarely one last time. And your mind might then very well use that as a weapon against you when it turns out that it wasn't your last time. The cycle of self-sabotage continues, and you'll simply continue beating yourself up over it until you consciously choose to do something differently.

Instead, what has a much greater chance of seeing you get to where you want to go is to give yourself the chance to start building trust in yourself by making one tiny promise. And then another tiny promise. And then another.

Start small, so as to not overwhelm the part of your brain that keeps you 'safe' from emotional discomfort via strategies to give you relief when things get hard.

Start imperfectly. This is almost the most important tip of all, because it's rare that the transition between an old habit and a new habit is wrinkle-free.

The most important tip of all? Start *now*.

Case study: Mira

Mira was hesitant to change. If you spoke to her, she'd tell you that she was 'addicted to being busy', even though her time before formal goal-setting was not being spent in ways that honoured her values. She had forecast that her future self would one day start doing the things that were important to her, but when it came to reshaping her schedule, she confessed to feeling nervous about letting go of the habit of procrastinating to do what she truly wanted to do, even when it was hard and the thought of scrolling news feeds for a while seemed preferable. She chose to start her time-blocked schedule on a Monday, because that's when her work week started. She didn't feel 'ready' on the Monday in question, though. Instead, she described feeling so frustrated with wasting her time up until that point that she was willing to try this new way of being, even with the small voice of doubt that accompanied her on Day 1.

Take a moment

Make some notes about how you'll move forward into your new way of being:

My action plan

My reasons for making this change are:

....

....

....

I can ask these people for help and support:

....

....

....

I need to remember that I am worthy, and . . .

....

....

....

I hereby give myself permission to try as many times as I need, and . . .

....

....

....

I will start (date, day, time):

....

....

....

The things I need are:

....

....

....

The people involved include:

....

....

....

I expect the first day I start to look like this (best-case scenario!):

....

....

....

I look forward to feeling these feelings:

....

....

....

I accept that I may feel discomfort that includes:

....

....

....

REMINDER: My values behind this change are:

....

....

....

I am going to share this plan with:

....

....

....

5

Creating and sustaining new habits

A habit is something that you make a conscious decision to do once, and then you stop thinking about because it's become automatic. Around 40 to 45 per cent of what we do every day is done out of habit. This means that almost half of our lives consist of behaviours that are repeated – the behaviours that we do over and over again that require very little cognitive or emotional effort from us because *it's just what we do*. Habits are behaviours that are ingrained in our neural pathways. They don't require much willpower because we've weaved them into the fabric of our daily lives. If you align your daily routines – that is, the 40 to 45 per cent of your day that's done by habit – with your values, then you improve the quality of your entire life.

The more you habitualise your life, the more willpower

you have left over to devote to demanding tasks. And this is why we're talking about habit creation and habit change as a pathway to living a bigger, better life. By taking the things that are aligned with who you want to be and making them into habits, and by changing habits that are sabotaging your efforts into habits that are self-supporting, the foundation of being who you want to be becomes more solid.

When self-sabotage happens more often than not in a particular area of your life, there's a likelihood that it's become ingrained as a habit. A habit of self-protection, helping you to avoid discomfort, to get relief from something difficult. Self-sabotaging habits create a disconnect between where we want to be and where we are. And even though it's agonising, because we'd much rather be on track, there's always a payoff that keeps us in this cycle. In other words, we become comfortable with the discomfort of being out of alignment with our values because it's safe and effortless.

The habit cycle

Human beings don't do things for no reason. There's always a need behind why you do what you do, even when you wish you would do something different.

The habit cycle unfolds like this: a cue or set of cues in your environment and/or within yourself occurs that triggers the brain to respond by choosing from a suite of automatic behaviours. Those behaviours are what we call routines. The cues determine which routine is chosen, and the brain essentially switches into automatic mode.

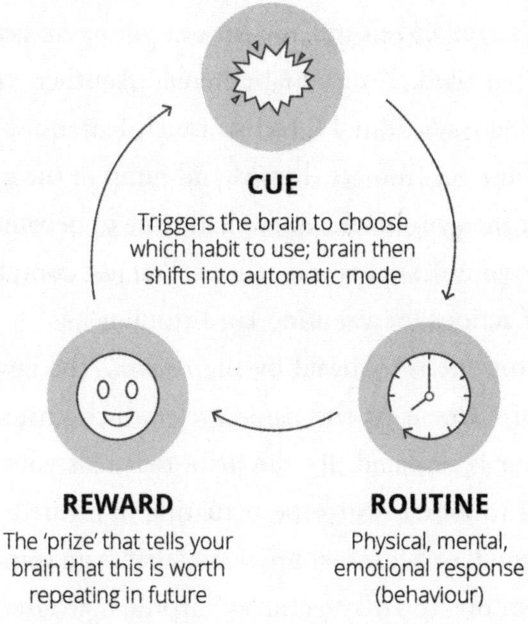
CUE
Triggers the brain to choose which habit to use; brain then shifts into automatic mode
REWARD
The 'prize' that tells your brain that this is worth repeating in future
ROUTINE
Physical, mental, emotional response (behaviour)

Let's say you have a habit of going to the gym each morning as soon as you wake up. One of your cues is that your alarm sounds at 5 am. You sit up and see your gym clothes and runners out ready for you to wear. This is another cue. You placed your drink bottle and towel out last night and they are already sitting beside your gym bag and your clothes. These are more cues.

The *routine* then occurs. This is where we carry out the automatic behaviour that the brain chooses in response to the cue. There might be physical, cognitive and emotional elements of the behaviour. You wake up to your alarm and sit up. You look at your gym gear and think, 'I'm tired. I can't be bothered.' Another thought arrives that says, 'But I'll feel so much better about my day if I just go.' You get dressed and jump in the car and arrive at the gym before you've had time to become fully aware of your thoughts and actions. You just completed a series of actions, or a routine, on autopilot.

The routine is followed by the *reward*. The reward is a crucial element of the habit cycle which ensures the behaviour is repeated. It's the prize that tells your brain that this routine is worth perpetuating in future because it feels good, or because it provided relief from some kind of discomfort. You may feel an endorphin high after going to the gym that boosts your mood. You might then drink your favourite smoothie for breakfast and feel a sense of accomplishment for going to the gym. Dopamine is released in the brain as part of this reward phase. It's a feel-good neurochemical that gives a sense of pleasure and motivation – that is, the motivation to repeat this behaviour next time those cues are present.

Going to the gym is an example of a self-supporting habit that might be consistent with being your best self. Let's look at the habit cycle when it relates to a self-defeating habit.

Self-defeating habit

You wake up and reach for your phone that's sitting in its charging dock beside your bed. It's proximity to you is a significant cue. Your partner asks you what you have on for the day, but you only half-heartedly answer because you're now three scrolls deep into your social media feeds. You're in the routine of scrolling before you've woken up properly. You walk to the kitchen and manage to leave your phone on the dining table while you make coffee. *Ding!* Another cue, and the phone is calling you back with the sound of an email. Your child wants to rehearse their talk for school that day, but you're well and truly into your inbox by now. Eyes fixed on the small screen in your hand, you half-nod at your daughter who presses on with her talk, used to competing with devices for your attention. The thought that you're not being the parent you want to be flits across your mind, but it's not strong enough to drown out the 'have to' thoughts that urgently demand you deal with work emails long before your day officially starts. You look up, and your daughter has disappeared to her room. You didn't hear her leave the kitchen because you were engrossed in the routine of immediately responding to emails. Despite some guilt about not being present for her, your brain rewards you with a dopamine download because the emails were done, plus an extra shot for the likes you received on your most recent post on Instagram. It's not who you want to be, but screen time seems to be your priority more and more these days. Most of the time, you're on your devices without even realising.

The thing about habits is that once the cues trigger the behaviour, our brains – quite literally – shift into autopilot mode. Far less conscious thought is required to carry out the behaviour and we have the experience of *doing it without thinking*.

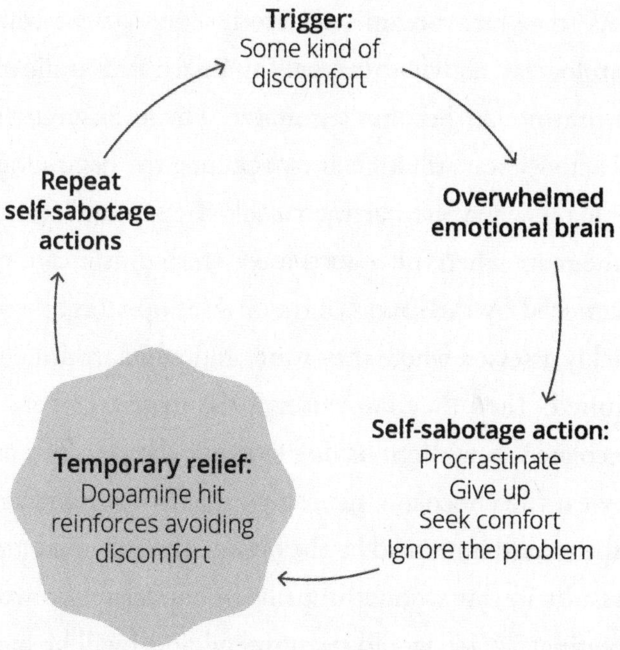

This has been studied in a fascinating experiment with rats. A divider clicks open and the rat enters a simple maze with chocolate as a reward at the end of the maze. The rats were identified as having high neurological activity when first entering and practising the maze. This means that as they entered the maze and explored their way through it to find the chocolate, there were many neurons firing in their brains. In other words, there was a lot of thinking they needed to do to navigate the maze initially.

As the rats became faster at solving the maze, neurological activity dropped dramatically, indicating the routine has become automatic. However, neurological activity was still high at two points: the beginning of the maze when the partition clicked open and the end of the maze when the reward was found. This means that when cued by the sound of the divider opening, the rats quickly assessed where they were, and which routine was required. Then they ran through the maze to where the chocolate was without having to think about it. But once they eat the chocolate, neurological activity spikes again as the reward is marked by the brain: 'This is a great maze! It results in this wonderful piece of chocolate! So worth repeating! 12/10, would recommend and I will be back!'

This demonstrates how habits require fewer cognitive resources from us than actions we don't do very often. Once something is made a habit, we don't have to think about it much. The more you habitualise in your life, the more willpower you have left over for difficult tasks.

This also means that if your day-to-day habits are unhelpful, or not taking you in a direction that you want to go, it feels easier to keep doing them rather than change them.

Once a behaviour is wired into our brains, those neural pathways don't disappear. We can't simply delete them, but we can build new neural pathways, and strengthen them so the new habits prevail over the old habits. We can interrupt that automatic behavioural cycle with awareness and decision-making to do something differently. This takes time, practice and patience, and always includes failure. The most successful habit-changers are the ones who have failed the most, or anticipated failure and prepared for it.

But first, we need to evaluate which habits are unhelpful, the cues that switch them on, and the rewards that keep them going.

Cues and rewards

Let's look at cues first. This might take some exploratory research and testing over a few days or weeks. There are five different types of cues:

- time of day
- the presence of certain people
- a particular place or environment
- an emotion
- and/or a preceding behaviour that has become ritualised.

It can be tricky to identify your cues because they are often subtle and occur outside of our awareness. For example, you reach for a cookie in the afternoon because it's 3 pm. You check your phone because it's right beside you.

When cues are present in multiples, the triggers for the habit are stronger. My dad is retired. He has a habit of napping each day. The cues for this are time, environment, emotion and, sometimes, a preceding behaviour.

The time is around 11 am. The environmental cues include a cup of tea, a book and a daybed on his veranda (my dad takes his day naps very seriously!). The emotion is usually a sense of calm and retreat preceded by satisfaction if he's completed a job that morning. And the preceding behaviour is usually some form of maintenance or hobby, like mowing the lawn or fixing something around the house. The strength of these cues contribute to my dad planning his day around his naps. A pretty good retirement if you ask me!

Stop and consider what the cues might be when it comes to a self-sabotaging habit that keeps showing up for you. Is there a consistent time of day that it occurs? Are there certain people present? Is there a common preceding emotion or thought that shows up? Does it occur in a particular place or environment? Does it follow the ritual of a preceding behaviour or event?

Now, let's look at rewards. What are the rewards that you're receiving from the self-sabotaging behaviour? If you're thinking, 'But wait, there is no reward! I don't want to self-sabotage at all!', then please remember that humans don't do things for no reason, even when those things push us further away from our values. The reward isn't always the addition of something pleasant to our day. Often, it's the removal or reduction of something unpleasant.

Take a moment

Consider the rewards of the unhelpful habit that you'd like to change. What are you getting out of it? What kind of discomfort is it helping you avoid, delay or reduce? What experience is it giving you that your emotional brain prefers over acting in line with your best self?

To replace your self-defeating habit with a self-supporting habit, you need to start with setting up the cues for the behaviour you want to be doing - the behaviour that is consistent with your values and being your best self. Make the cues as obvious as possible. The more cues you set up for the habit, the stronger the neural pathways become to ritualise the behaviour. Our brains are very motivated to complete a habit cycle, so when a cue is present – even if it's subtle – the brain still wants to follow through the old habit cycle to the point of completion. Removing the cues for unhelpful habits decreases the risk of those triggers activating the old behaviour pattern of self-sabotage.

Along with setting up cues, the most important thing you can do for establishing new self-supporting habits is to choose salient rewards. Choose your rewards ahead of time and make sure they are actually rewarding. This might sound obvious, but if the reward isn't something that makes us highly motivated – at least initially – then it simply doesn't work as well to reinforce a behaviour. It's also more effective to plan an extrinsic reward initially. That is, the reward comes from outside yourself. Eventually, with practice and repetition, the reward for the behaviour becomes intrinsic.

Sarah's story

Sarah was studying to become a nurse. Sarah experienced her most productive hours in the evening after dinner. This is when she felt brightest and most focused. But instead of studying, Sarah complained that she spent her time watching TV and scrolling social media on her phone. This habit was affecting the amount of time she devoted to study. It created a pattern of Sarah being unfocused and exhausted by the time she hit the books, and then getting to bed later than planned. She was constantly playing catch up.

There were a number of cues that triggered this habit for Sarah. The TV was in the middle of her living room, where she also tended to sit with her textbooks. She always had her phone near her hand, or close by on the coffee table, as well as the TV remote. The feeling of being satisfied after dinner also triggered a feeling of relaxation, which Sarah associated with Netflix and relaxing. Sarah also turned the lights down when she was watching TV and scrolling on her phone, so the low light triggered a mellow response rather than encouraging focused activity.

The routine started after she washed up from dinner. She moved to the lounge, turned the lights down, picked up the remote to switch the TV on, and began scrolling on her phone. The reward for this routine was that she successfully delayed the brainpower and effort of studying when she didn't feel like it. Even though this habit messed with her sleep routine and meant that she fell behind in her study plan, the routine continued because her brain marked relaxing as preferred over the effort of studying. Remember that emotional brains will always choose comfort over discomfort until we train our elephants otherwise. Half-watching Netflix while scrolling social media on her phone did not bring a host of positive emotions with it, because Sarah was constantly wrestling with the guilt over not studying. It was the relief of delaying the cognitive effort of studying that kept her procrastination routine in a cycle of repetition each evening.

Sarah wanted to study for one hour in the evenings from 7 pm until 8 pm daily from Monday through to Friday. We worked on a combination of adding cues for her study habit and removing cues for her TV and social media-scrolling habit.

After she finished washing up in the evening, she sat down at her desk in her office rather than moving to the lounge. She placed her phone in a drawer in her bedroom, far away from her reach. She left the lights on throughout the house instead of turning them down. She did not switch the TV on. She wore headphones and listened to playlists of low-fi beats, music that she associated with being focused.

Let's look at how rewards worked for Sarah. Sarah didn't enjoy studying. The act of studying was important to her overarching goal of having a career that she was passionate about but studying itself was not a reward. Because she didn't like it, we could not rely on the habit of studying to be reinforcing. Instead, when Sarah started dismantling her procrastination habit in favour of replacing it with studying, three extrinsic rewards were introduced. The first reward was four squares of dark chocolate with almonds through it – Sarah's favourite kind of chocolate. She ate these squares throughout the study hour. The second reward was the satisfaction of a timer. Sarah purchased a one-hour hourglass timer and placed it on her desk. The final reward was – you guessed it – Netflix! After the hour was up, Sarah moved to the lounge, switched on the TV and grabbed her phone. Eventually, she found that the satisfaction of getting her study done meant that she enjoyed her TV time more, and that it had flow-on effects to reduce her time scrolling on her phone. She also experienced a deep sense of relief from the guilt of not studying that had been plaguing her when she was procrastinating, and better sleep, too! The rewards for Sarah's new way of being had become intrinsic.

Make sure the reward happens quickly after your new routine or behaviour so that your brain begins reinforcing this new workable and helpful set of actions. The reason that this is important is that your brain craves the reward that self-sabotage has been giving you. Think about the craving for relief of whatever discomfort your self-sabotage has been helping you avoid. Your success at overcoming self-sabotage to create new habits dramatically increases when you plan for the cravings to continue, but prepare to meet them in a different way – as opposed to hoping the cravings will disappear, being unprepared for them, and then having them take over when they show up.

INTRODUCING NEW HABITS

SELF-SUPPORTING ACTION

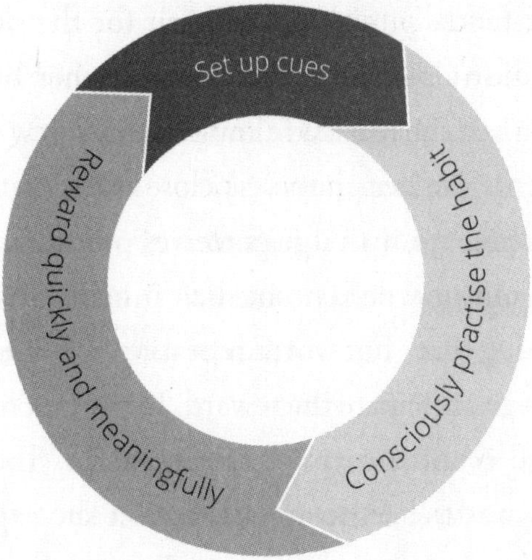

Eventually, the habit begins to happen automatically in response to the cues, and the rewards shift to being intrinsic

Sarah still craved the chance to relax her brain, so immediately after studying, she met that craving the way she always had. When you take the time to reward yourself for a new, self-supporting behaviour, your brain marks that behaviour as something that feels good and is therefore worth repeating. This helps to cultivate our sense of self-belief that we can develop and sustain new self-supporting habits in place of old, unhelpful habits.

If you don't set up the new habit well – that is, the cues and rewards are not effective – then you run the risk of inadvertently punishing yourself for the new habit. If Sarah didn't plan for a way to relax her brain after studying, then she may have continued to view study as a punishment. The brain pays very close attention to rewards and punishments, and if it perceives punishment as the result of your new behaviour, then it marks that routine as something that's not worth repeating. We need to train our brains to anticipate the reward. In the first few weeks, the reward is still a surprise for our brain. The surprise for Sarah was the sense of satisfaction she experienced from studying, rather than the guilt of procrastinating. Conscious attention to the new behaviour and reward helps to attach those two things together and encourages our brains to mark this routine as one to habitualise.

Take a moment

Identify the cues and rewards for your self-defeating habit, then set up cues and rewards for your self-supporting habit. Remember that the closer you can make your rewards to the rewards that have kept the self-sabotage continuing, the better! The brain is more willing to do something new if the reward is the same, or similar, or just as good.

Use the worksheet that follows to identify your cues and rewards. It may take some investigation over a few days or weeks before you have identified all of them, so give yourself the time and space to get curious about this habit and what prompts it to occur and repeat.

The cues for my self-sabotage are:

Time of day:

....

Place:

....

People:

....

Feelings:

....

A preceding behaviour(s):

....

The rewards for my self-sabotage are:

....
....
....
....
....
....
....
....
....
....
....
....
....
....
....
....
....
....
....
....
....
....
....
....

When you start a new habit, be mindful that there's a honeymoon phase. It seems easy and there's a seductive spike in motivation, but this only lasts until some form of stress occurs to disrupt your routine.

Sarah was studying every day for the first week. In the second week, her best friend experienced a relationship breakup and stayed the night at Sarah's on Tuesday. This interrupted her study routine. When something like this happens during the formation of a new habit, the brain copes by returning to what's familiar. On Wednesday night, even though Sarah's friend had returned home, Sarah washed the dishes after dinner and then moved to the lounge with her phone in hand and turned Netflix on. Rather than go to her desk to study, Sarah did what she'd always done. This is how it gets harder before it gets easier.

Case study: Mira

Self-sabotage in the form of procrastination had become a habit for Mira. Environmental cues that prompted her to procrastinate included having her phone in her line of sight, having news sites as permanent tabs in her browser, and any unexpected interruption to her work tasks: e.g. the musical conclusion of the washing machine cycle, a knock at the door from a delivery driver, her dog needing to go outside - and then asking to come back inside, etc. Mira is a morning person, so attempting to focus after lunchtime was a more vulnerable period for procrastination (time of day cue). Feeling bored, overwhelmed, stressed or facing an undesired or difficult work task prompted procrastination (emotional cues). And Mira's procrastination was guaranteed whenever there was a notification which pulled her away from one screen and onto another: e.g. email, group messaging and calendar notifications. The *ding* of a notification and diversion of her attention was a ritualised behaviour cue that prompted procrastination.

The rewards for her procrastination were primarily the removal of discomfort - she was relieved of having to do a difficult, boring or otherwise undesired work task. Sometimes, the reward was a false positive - the feeling of satisfying productivity from cleaning, for example. For a short period of time, it feels good, until the guilt sets in about the tasks that were supposed to be done in that timeframe instead.

Mira committed to removing her phone from

the room altogether during the time blocks in her schedule where she was prone to being interrupted. She used it during meditation because she liked a particular app with calming music, and she used it during work admin time to post on social media. But during deep work, painting and time with her son, Mira put her phone in a kitchen drawer so that it was more difficult to access. She removed the tabs for news sites from her browser, and blocked them from being able to be accessed at all during certain times in her day. While unexpected interruptions can't be avoided altogether, Mira committed to using the Pomodoro technique, which allowed her to plan certain interruptions for her short break periods. Let the dog out during the break. Hang the washing out during the break, etc.

We worked on keeping the rewards the same, but reframed them to be values-led. Rather than seeking quick and easy productivity (e.g. cleaning), Mira practised reminding herself that the satisfaction of alignment with her values (i.e. sticking to her time blocks) was unbeatable. We built the relief that Mira was seeking into her day via small breaks. It's much easier to keep going when you replenish yourself during the day.

Take a moment

Now take a moment to consider the cues and rewards you could set up to introduce your self-supporting habit:

The cues for my self-supporting habit could be:

Time of day:

....

Place:

....

People:

....

Feelings:

....

A preceding behaviour(s):

....

The rewards for my self-supporting habit could be:

....
....
....
....
....
....
....
....
....
....
....
....
....
....
....
....
....
....
....
....
....
....

6

Replenishing your willpower bucket

Asking your brain to replace an old, self-defeating habit with a new self-supporting habit means asking it to work harder for a while. It means asking it to not just drive on a different neural highway, but to construct that new highway in the first place. This takes willpower.

> **Willpower is how much inner strength you have available to carry out a difficult task. It's the collective sum of your cognitive resources, which include your attention, concentration, mental energy, emotional energy, physical energy, and your perception of how psychologically strong you feel.**

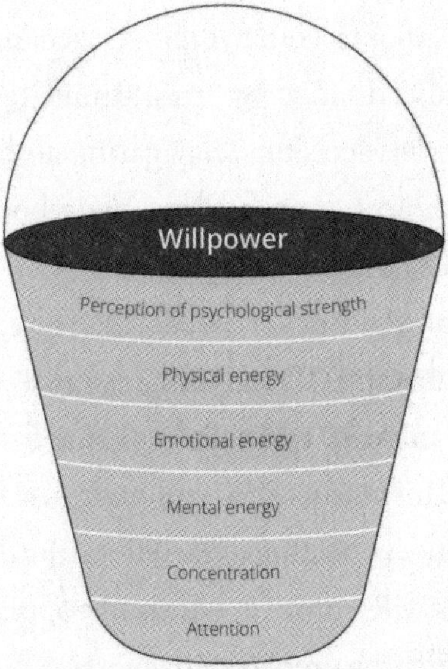

When it comes to dismantling old habits and creating new habits, these new routines drain your willpower. Plentiful stores of willpower are essential for making any change.

Think of willpower like a bucket that can be filled. Assuming all things are equal and you've slept well and are not under any additional stress, your willpower bucket starts full at the beginning of the day. This is when you have maximum attention, concentration, energy and perception of psychological strength.

Your willpower bucket is drained throughout the day. Your resources reduce as the demands of the day use them up. The greater number of challenging tasks you set yourself, the quicker your willpower gets depleted. Your willpower is also drained by stress, multi-tasking, having to make complex decisions, navigating an overwhelming number of choices, not fuelling your body and mind effectively, and fatigue.

Your willpower bucket needs to be replenished for optimal functioning. Once your resources are depleted, they will not increase again unless some form of restoration occurs. This means that you can't just keep working through it, and expecting yourself to do difficult tasks, hoping things will improve, without stopping for a break to give yourself a chance to rejuvenate.

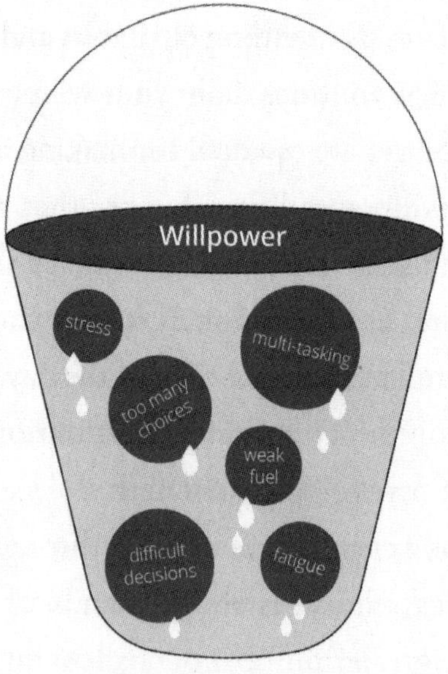

Expanding your bucket

The good news is that your willpower capacity is not fixed. It can be built up over time, so that you start each day with a little more in your bucket.

Living a bigger life means that you honour yourself by treating yourself respectfully and kindly. You are worth it. You deserve to live into the potential of being the version of you that you desire. Creating small habits to support who you are becoming is about having the patience to dislodge and rewrite old stories that we carry about ourselves into new stories of empowerment. It's about cultivating the habits to support this new identity. This takes time and consistent, tiny actions towards the life we want for ourselves, and to take these tiny steps and actions, we need willpower. The most consequential thing you can do for your present and future success with new habits is to cultivate your willpower and replenish your bucket.

When you're changing habits, you can't expect yourself to follow through on doing anything differently if you start with an empty bucket. Remember that low cognitive resources equals low willpower, and low willpower equals your brain returning to what's easy and automatic, even if those things are not in alignment with being your best self.

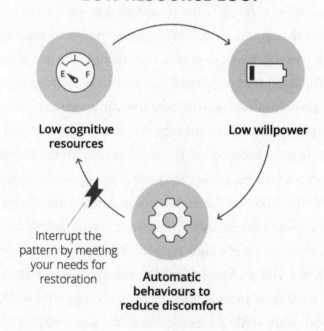

If you're serious about stepping into your potential, then get serious about filling your willpower bucket. Because the more you nourish and build up your resources, the stronger you'll be to choose a self-supporting alternative instead of old self-sabotage routines.

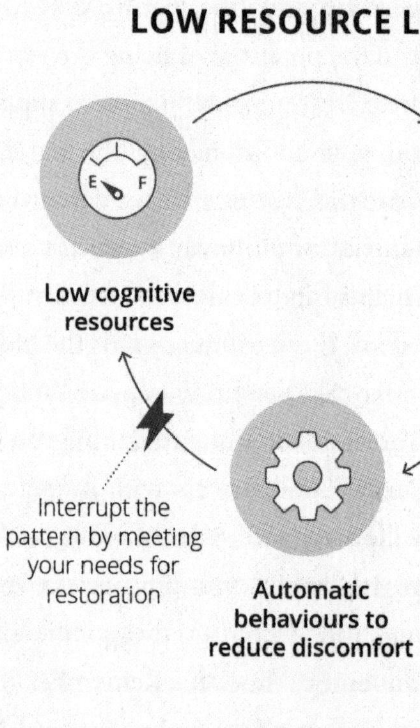

LOW RESOURCE LOOP

Interrupt the pattern by meeting your needs for restoration

Tony's story

Tony was in his early 30s and working in a corporate position that placed a significant amount of stress on his shoulders. He came to me for help with low mood. He was feeling mildly depressed as a result of his life becoming unbalanced. Almost all his energy was spent working. The remainder of the time, he simply rested so he had enough energy to return to work the following week. He'd lost touch with anything he did for enjoyment, his relationships were suffering, and he was concerned that he was on a path that was causing him to feel deeply unhappy.

Working for the majority of his waking hours had become a habit for Tony. As long as he was working, he convinced himself that he would get to the point where his in-tray would be empty and then he could and would relax. The problem was that it never happened. His in-tray was never-ending, and his schedule didn't spontaneously open up for him to take some time to chill out.

It may surprise you, but Tony's initial focus was not on bringing more enjoyment and relaxation into his life. While this is what he needed, when stress is already present, attempting to change habits at the same time can quickly drain what willpower is left after accounting for the willpower needed to cope with the stress. By the time he waded through his inbox of around 200 daily emails, and fielded tens of missed calls from his team managing urgent issues, there was little left in Tony's tank for his own work tasks, let alone his personal life. We started by looking at strategies that Tony could use to respond more effectively to the stress in his workplace. He had an honest conversation with his manager about the unreasonable workload he was expected to handle and his manager agreed to redistribute some of his tasks to other members of the team. Tony also used his exceptional engineering skills to automate a number of his work tasks to free him up to respond to crises – which was his main role. And finally, Tony practised reframing the pressure he put on himself to complete everything, every day. Once he felt more in control of his workload and had changed his perspective about what must be done in a day in order for him to feel competent and worthy, we then moved to creating new habits outside of work for enjoyment and relaxation. Tony was an avid hiker and outdoorsman. He reconnected with hiking during the week, leaving work earlier to take short hikes on a couple of afternoons. He set a long-term goal to climb several mountain peaks in Colorado, USA, and began training with a mate for this adventure. And he introduced ten minutes of meditation each morning before he left for work, and each evening before he went to bed.

Once his willpower bucket was back to a sufficient level for habit change and the stress wasn't leaving it constantly drained, he was able to learn to do things differently to live more purposefully. Not bad for a man who told me he was, 'Too old to change my ways'!

Filling your bucket

We cultivate cognitive resources by paying attention to our needs, seeking to fulfil those needs in a healthy way, and working with and not against ourselves. Cognitive resources can be maintained (and improved!) during the day by doing the following things.

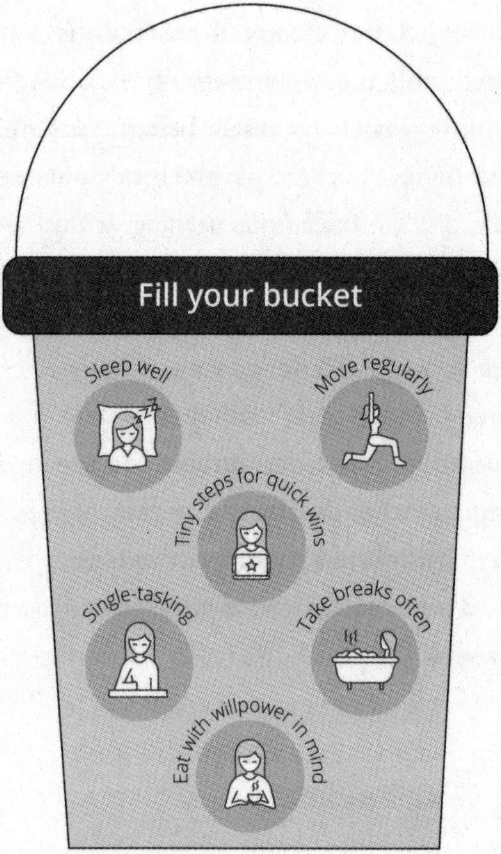

Look after your body. Keep to a sleep schedule that gives you plenty of quality rest, and prioritise time for movement so that your body receives a chance to release tension, especially if you sit for long periods during the day. Even a five-minute walk in between tasks can build willpower stores. Also, ensure you have adequate nutritional intake and hydration during the day. If your body is not firing on all cylinders, willpower is drained more quickly.

Don't overwhelm yourself before you even start. Approach big goals by breaking them down into small goals. If a task on your list is too big, it can overwhelm even a full willpower bucket and leave you feeling drained and demotivated. Break the task down into consecutive small goals, and then watch your willpower be replenished as you tick off each small task.

Practise single-tasking. Although multi-tasking can feel tempting, and convince you that you're achieving more, it actually means that your output will generally be lower in quality and your willpower ends up being heavily taxed. Obviously there are times when you will stir the sauce for dinner with the baby on your hip, while discussing the mortgage repayments with your partner and calling your toddler away from pressing Play Doh into the carpet. The fear of 'dropping the ball' is real. But it is not necessarily *accurate*. Single-tasking offers the chance to train our focus, increasing the efficiency and effectiveness of getting things done.

Plan and take regular breaks throughout the day. Taking a short break between tasks helps to give your brain a chance to relax and reset. Make time for relaxation – and I don't mean housework, or food prep, or anything else that might be something you tick off your list as a 'thing that must be done'. I mean relaxation that is deeply restorative, whatever that is for you. It might be reading, or sitting in the sun, or catching up with friends, or walking in nature. Schedule in mental downtime to enhance creativity, problem solving and general wellbeing. This time is where you don't ask your brain to do much at all, and you simply allow yourself to be.

Kat's story

When Kat came to see me to address her stress levels, she described carrying a greater burden of cognitive load for household management and parenting than her husband. She was convinced that if she didn't multi-task, then the flow of things would fall apart. Kat's concerns are not unique; she is one of the great majority of parents who are trying to do it all, and all at once.

Kat started using project management software as her primary organisation tool and set it up to remind her of all the recurring tasks for her family. She communicated the perceived weight of her load to her husband - a load, it turned out, that he didn't realise was affecting her so much. He began participating more actively, also using the program as a prompt for what needed to be done and when. But the most powerful change for Kat was altering her expectations. By giving herself permission to be beautifully and imperfectly human, her relationship with productivity changed. Tasks were completed mindfully, without trying to do everything at once. Her stress was no longer affecting her wellbeing.

Go for quick wins. This doesn't mean that you need to be perfect, or give up managing the multiple demands and needs of those around you altogether. Instead, there are two tools you can use for some quick wins. One: revise your expectations. This might be less than palatable if you thrive on productivity, but the hard truth is that you are not superhuman, and your willpower capacity relies on you remembering your humanness. Be mindful that you can only ask so much of yourself at once, and that it's a strength to ask for help.

Two: use memory prompts to reduce your cognitive load. The same number of things might need doing, but by using a to-do list, reminders on your phone or calendar, or visual reminders like fridge notes, you can save your willpower for the tasks themselves rather than the strain of attempting to remember each of those tasks time and again.

Dopamine hits

Cultivating cognitive resources also includes doing things that result in a release of dopamine, that feel-good neurochemical responsible for rewarding actions that are then marked as being worthy of repeating and therefore making into habits.

There are things you can do to increase the release of dopamine during the day. First, try doing the hardest thing on your to-do list at the start of the day. I often do this if I have a task that I don't particularly like doing, or a task that is going to take a lot of brainpower, like writing a book! Getting the task over and done with first thing in the morning provides a huge release of dopamine which can actually increase the willpower you have available for the rest of the day.

I'm a big fan of crossing off tasks as they are completed. This simple act gives a spike of dopamine. Watch your willpower skyrocket as you can actually see the documented results of your productivity.

The same goes for keeping a promise to yourself. Let's say you want to develop a habit of walking each morning. You make a promise to yourself that you'll start tomorrow, at 7 am. Tomorrow comes around, it's 7 am, and despite the effort involved, you keep your promise by getting dressed and going on your walk. The dopamine release from the satisfaction of keeping that promise to yourself, as well as from the exercise, will fill your willpower bucket.

You can also create a dopamine release to help you keep going through the day by acknowledging your wins, no matter how small. Self-encouragement builds cognitive resources by tapping into your emotional energy and reminding you of how far you have come.

Try to minimise stress. Remember that you are just one person, and as much as you might wish you were, you're not superhuman, and nor should you expect yourself to be. Having said this, it's not reasonable to plan as if life won't continue to happen. It will, and things that demand your attention and throw you off balance will show up, no matter how determined you are to start a new habit.

This is when your brain will want to return to the old routines and self-defeating behaviours, because they provide relief and they are familiar. The neural pathways for these routines are well-worn. During this phase of getting off track and then bringing yourself back on track, your willpower will be drained quickly. That's why it's important to reduce decision-making by setting up effective cues. If you can turn a chore into a choice and you feel in control of making the decision to do something differently, your brain will release dopamine and you'll feel a spike in motivation. We need to decide what the new behaviour will be and then reduce the decision-making around that behaviour as much as possible, to conserve willpower.

Willingness and discipline are key factors, too. The willingness to change is about being so uncomfortable with your present reality that the discomfort of change is preferable to staying stuck in your self-sabotaging habits. Discipline is the act of making tiny choice after tiny choice to continue to come back into alignment with your values, even when it's hard, and even when you have to start over and over again.

Willingness is a mindset; discipline is the actions you take based on that mindset. Willpower helps you stay willing and disciplined.

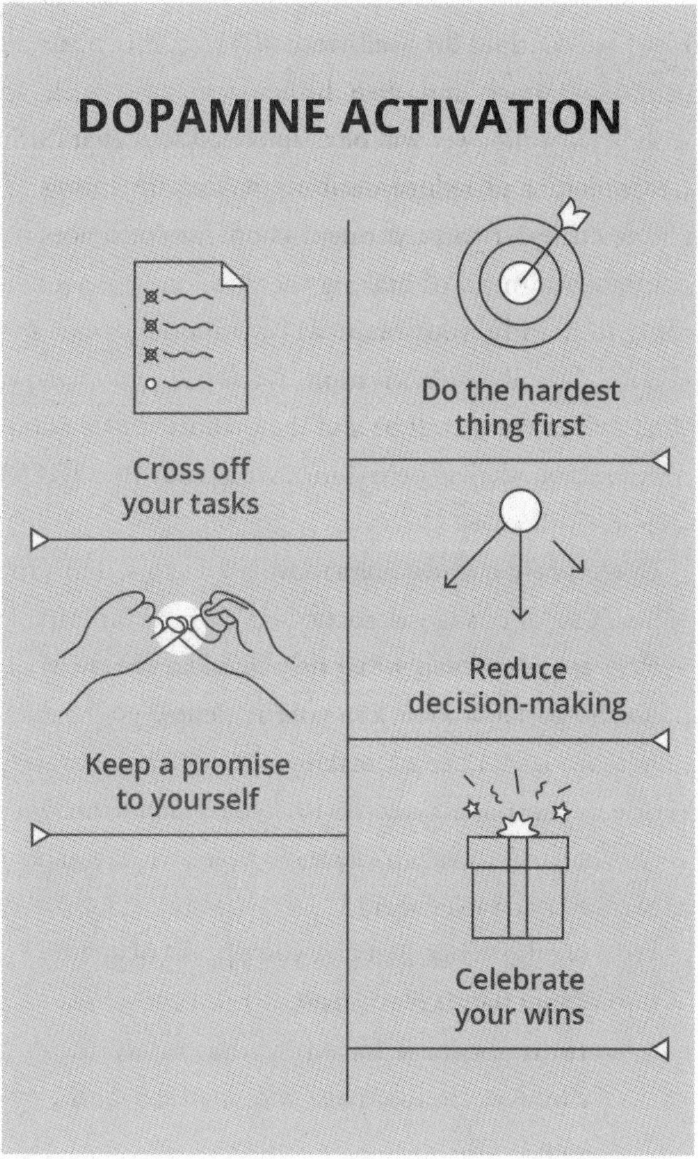
DOPAMINE ACTIVATION
Cross off your tasks
Do the hardest thing first
Reduce decision-making
Keep a promise to yourself
Celebrate your wins

Take a moment

It is time to be radically honest about what's draining your willpower bucket. Include things that are external to you and things you're doing, or not doing.

....

....

....

....

Now, consider these questions:

How are you doing with basic building blocks of functioning (nutrition, movement, sleep)?

....

....

....

What are the things that give you a boost of energy throughout the day?

....

....

....

What are the things you are doing to manage stress?

....

....

....

Do you tend to try and multi-task, or have you mastered the art of single-tasking?

....

....

....

Now, write down one thing you could start doing to help fill up your willpower bucket. Start small. Kat started using project management software. You might take a five-minute break every half an hour. Or have snacks and water nearby to keep your energy stable. Quick wins are where the magic happens for new habits.

....

....

....

....

....

Case study: Mira

Mira was surprised at how much she had expected of herself without paying any attention to her stores of willpower. Once she acknolwedged that she was a morning person, she could work with her circadian rhythms rather than against them. She started doing her hardest tasks at the beginning of the day to align with her energy levels. She adjusted her nutrition habits by reducing caffeine and eating at regular times, and she scheduled in short breaks to give herself space to decompress throughout the day. Mira reported feeling more stable in her emotions and energy, and found it easier to switch on for work and switch off for her personal life.

7

Managing uncomfortable feelings

Humans are wired to avoid discomfort at all costs, and avoidance of discomfort can become so ingrained that, one day, you wake up to find your life is shaped by habits of self-sabotage rather than habits that are in the service of living by your values. And this is not where you wanted to be. At all.

This is your responsibility to manage, but it's not your *fault*. Your biology influences these patterns of avoidance because avoidance of discomfort was once essential for survival. Our culture also has a large role to play here, and your elephant is hard to ignore when it decides to rampage!

Toxic happiness

Our culture's obsession with happiness makes our day-to-day experience of emotions confusing. Of the primary emotions that we experience – love, joy, surprise, fear, sadness, anger, disgust and shame – over half are uncomfortable. And yet we are socialised to believe that if we have uncomfortable feelings, there must be something wrong with us.

Western culture will have you believe that you can purchase, strive and achieve your way to happiness. That through the acquisition of a big house, a fancy car, a high income to support your lifestyle, climbing the career ladder to status and power after completing your university education, while you wear the right clothing labels in the right dress size, as well as having a perfect marriage and 2.4 children, you'll be perfectly and permanently happy.

We assume that everyone else has their lives sorted out and there's something missing for us when we don't. We assume that our uncomfortable feelings are problematic, that we are defective because we are not happy all the time. And we seek to get rid of the pain, change the pain, or avoid it at all costs. You only need to look at the fact that we have a divorce rate of around one in three, and a culture of addiction, consumerism and need-it-now attitudes to see people avoiding their pain.

Avoidance

Because you've been a human all your life, you know that uncomfortable feelings are part of the ride. Avoiding them is not working for you, because it only leads you to have more pain in the long-term, even if it does give initial short-term relief.

Avoidance means that, eventually, the quality of our lives deteriorates because our comfort zones get smaller and smaller.

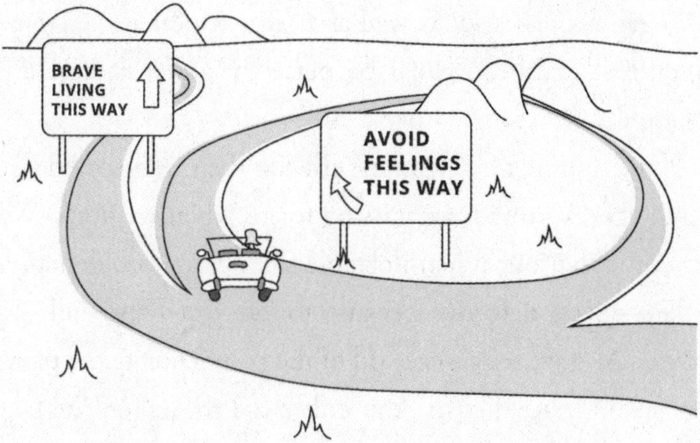

What you may not realise is that the discomfort that we experience is often in direct proportion to how much we care about something. The more you value something, the more pain you'll experience when the thing that you care about doesn't work out, or goes wrong, or doesn't materialise, or leaves, or becomes a source of misalignment.

Your self-defeating habits cause you significant levels of emotional pain because they represent what you don't want to be. They represent a life that is not consistent with your best self. Your emotional discomfort is a messenger that is offering you an invitation back to a path that's headed in the direction of the things you care about most, who you want to be as a person, and what you want to stand for.

RELATIONSHIP BETWEEN WHAT YOU VALUE AND THE DISCOMFORT YOU FEEL

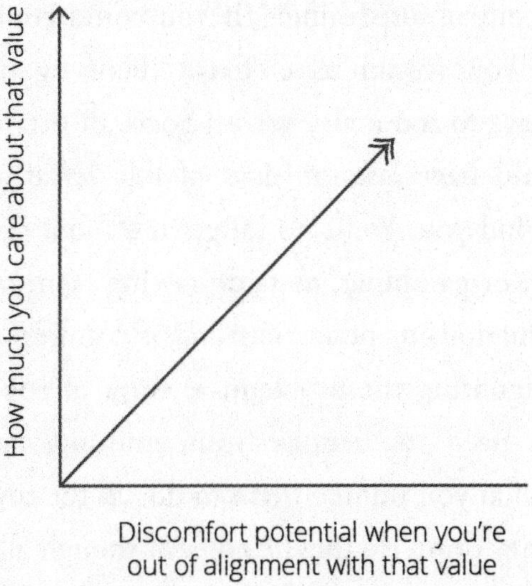

Just because you know about emotional discomfort doesn't mean you like it, want it or approve of it. What it does mean is that you need to find a way to accept it in the service of living a bigger, better life.

Your mind may not be convinced. After all, why can't we just turn our feelings off? Surely, there must be a way, right?

Well, you could try not caring about the things that you currently care about, but soon enough, the feelings will return. Which is lucky, because the richness of life is found in its colour, not in numbing out or shutting down. And we also have the small problem of not being able to control our feelings. If you could control your feelings, you would have 'fixed' them by now. You would have found a way to feel good all the time, and you would have left the days of self-defeating habits long behind you. You'd no longer use food, or alcohol, or drugs, or gambling, or withdrawing from others, or procrastination, or perfectionism, or blaming everyone else, or ignoring the problem, as ways of coping. You wouldn't need to, because your emotions would do exactly what you wanted them to do, all the time.

But they don't, do they? And even though all of those coping strategies work briefly, the discomfort comes back, doesn't it?

We can't directly control our feelings. Sure, we can influence them, but we can't rely on being able to control when they show up, how long they last, and when they pass.

The better news is that feelings don't control us.

Take a moment

Think of a time when you did something that made you feel really scared. You might have given a speech in front of a lot of people, or you might have driven a car for the first time, or gone for a job interview, or jumped out of a plane. If fear or any other uncomfortable emotion really controlled us, then you wouldn't have been able to do any of those things.

So, if we can't control our feelings, what can we control? You can control your *actions*. It is what you do that is within your control. No matter what you feel or think, you can still take action in line with your values to do what matters. This is why Nike uses the slogan 'Just Do It', and not, 'Just Do It When You Feel Good', or 'Just Do It When You Feel Like It', or 'Just Do It When All Your Emotional Ducks Are In A Row And Everyone Agrees With You And Your Great-Uncle Has Promised You A Hefty Inheritance For Being Your Brilliant Self'. We can control how we respond to our feelings. Rather than letting our feelings dictate what we do, we can learn to accept discomfort in the service of taking action that's aligned with our values. That means that we can learn to sit with a feeling and not react in an avoidant way to that feeling.

Emotional awareness

Your power lies in how you choose to respond; in your skills of emotional awareness.

Emotional awareness is the practice of observing feelings as they show up, particularly in the space between a trigger and our response to that trigger. It's in this space that we have a choice: face the feeling directly, or run away from it, avoid it, numb it, or try to change it in some way.

When it comes to habits, remember that our brains essentially shut down in the middle of the habit cycle when they are performing the routine. In this autopilot mode, we don't pay attention to how we feel when we're doing it. We're in a state of mindlessness. This means that your self-defeating habits could have you repeatedly doing things that you *don't really like doing* and things that don't make you feel good, but you're not aware of it because the nature of a habit is that we don't pay much attention while we're doing it.

You don't have to have all your emotional ducks in a row before you start doing what's important to you. Change is created the minute you do one thing differently. If you're feeling a little overwhelmed with the idea of feeling your feelings, stop and give yourself a moment to catch your breath. It can feel confronting to think about sitting with feelings you've spent a long time avoiding. Work through this step by step. Small steps lead to big wins when it comes to changing habits.

Take a moment

Let's dive into how we accept uncomfortable feelings in the service of moving towards growth. We're going to follow a process of observing without judgement, using breath as a connection to grounding, giving yourself permission to be in the feeling, and allowing it to be what it is, rather than making your feelings right or wrong.

This exercise might feel foreign at first, but most things feel clunky the first time you try them. Please give yourself the chance to try it out, because your freedom from emotional paralysis and self-defeating habits is on the other side.

If you can, and feel comfortable to do so, gently close your eyes or let your gaze soften at a spot nearby. Get in touch with the emotion that you're experiencing right now. If you're not feeling anything particularly uncomfortable, take yourself back to a time recently when you did experience a painful feeling. Allow yourself to get in touch with that feeling for the purposes of this exercise. As you learn to do this exercise in your daily life, you'll call on this tool as the uncomfortable feeling occurs in real time.

Get in touch with the emotion as much as you possibly can. Now open your eyes, and take a couple of moments to find the feeling in your body.

1. If you could locate this feeling in your body, where would it be?

   ....

   ....

2. If you could trace an outline around this feeling, as if it were an object in your body, what shape would it have?

   ....

   ....

3. How big is the feeling? How much of that part of your body is it taking up?

   ....

   ....

4. Does the feeling have a weight?

   ....

   ....

5. Does the feeling have a temperature?

   ....

   ....

6. What colour is the feeling?

   ....

   ....

7. Is it moving, or is it still?

    ....

    ....

8. What kind of texture does the feeling have on the outside?

    ....

    ....

9. What kind of texture does it have on the inside?

    ....

    ....

10. What kind of substance is the feeling made of?

    ....

    ....

11. If the feeling had a power, say out of ten, where ten is most intense, how would you rate the intensity of the feeling right now?

    ....

    ....

Here's some space to draw your feeling to help you visualise how you experience it in your body.

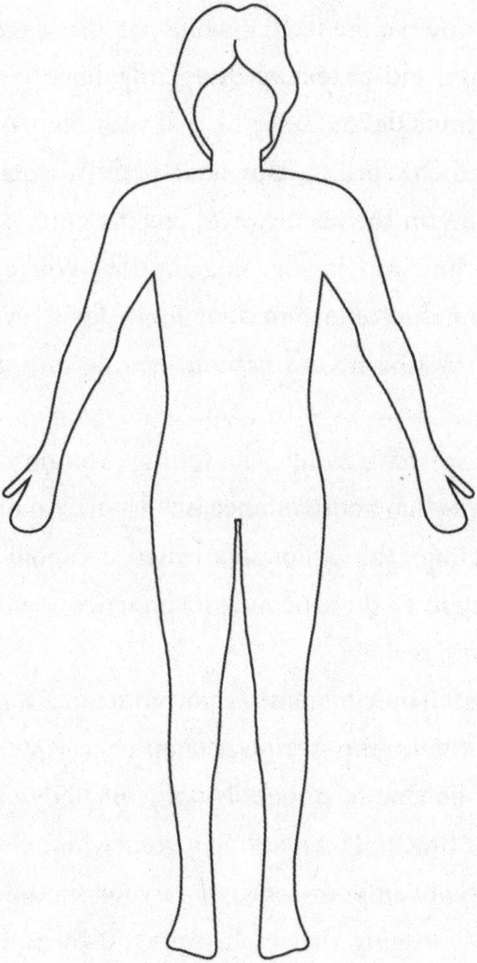

Remember to approach this with curiosity. There are no right or wrong answers; just consider the answer that your mind gives you first.

Now, observe the feeling while you bring your attention to your breath. Breathe in gently, breathe out fully. With each inhalation, imagine that your body is opening up around the feeling, that your body is expanding to make room for the feeling. And breathe out.

Each time you inhale, imagine that you're opening up around the feeling, making room for it to be there without resisting it, and without getting into a struggle with it.

You don't have to like the feeling. You don't have to want the feeling and you certainly don't have to approve of the feeling. This is not about that. It's about allowing the feeling to be there because its presence is valid simply because you feel it.

With each breath, make a little more room for it. If you find that the feeling is in your chest or in your stomach, you may be able to physically see your body expanding with your breath. If the feeling is somewhere else in your body, perhaps in your arms, or in your shoulders, or in your legs, imagine that each time you breathe in, that this part of your body is expanding to make room for the feeling to be there.

Watch for any judgements that your mind might be bringing up, and then let them go. This is not about judging the feeling. It's about accepting it unconditionally. This is not about getting rid of the feeling, or making the feeling something different. It's purely about using your breath to give the feeling space to be present in whatever way, shape or form the feeling is showing up for you right now.

What was your relationship like with the feeling at the start of that exercise? What was the intensity of the feeling like at the start of the exercise? And what is the intensity of the feeling like now at the end of the exercise? You might find that by allowing the feeling to be present, its intensity actually decreases, or, at least, doesn't worsen.

Comparatively, when we fight with our feelings, the energy of the struggle feeds the feeling and tends to intensify it further. This is about rewiring those neural pathways in your brain to be able to transform your relationship with discomfort so it doesn't keep you stuck.

The more you can practise this exercise, the better. Initially, you might find that a quiet, undisturbed place is the best way for you to practise accepting your discomfort. With more practice, you'll become more comfortable with observing your feelings in this way and be able

MANAGING UNCOMFORTABLE FEELINGS

STEP 1 Describe the feeling or discomfort in as much detail as possible, with curiosity and without judgement.

STEP 2 Go to your breath and imagine your body making space around the feeling.

STEP 3 Commit to carrying the feeling exactly as it is, without struggling with it or trying to get rid of it.

STEP 4 Let it be, or let it go, if it passes.

STEP 5 Take values-directed action. Come back to what's important, right here and right now.

Case study: Mira

Mira learned to sit with the feelings that she would usually band-aid with procrastination. The most frequent emotion she identified as problematic for her was overwhelm at how many things she perceived she had to do each day. Sitting with the overwhelm, rather than fighting it or trying to overcome it with more productivity, counterintuitively offered Mira the space to respond more calmly. Being organised is much easier when it comes from a place of ease rather than force!

8

How to handle unhelpful thoughts

Your subconscious mind's job is to keep you safe. The chatter that keeps you firmly ensconced in your comfort zone is the expression of what your brain is wired to do. Your job is to respond to your mind effectively. Ideally, you do that in a way that allows you to evaluate what it's telling you. I'd suggest using a liberal dose of curiosity and a commitment to not take it too seriously. But why is it so difficult to do?

Our minds have evolved over thousands of years to be survival machines. It was highly adaptive for our ancestors to act when their minds warned of all the potential problems that existed which could be threatening to life. Our ancestors' minds were fixated on quandaries like the next available source of food and water, adequate shelter, weapons, and forms of protection for themselves and their group. They were also focused on maintaining belonging and connection to the group and managing threats from predators and rival groups.

Our minds are inherently linked to our survival response – the fight/flight/freeze response – because of the way we have evolved. If a problem is detected, the fight/flight/freeze response is triggered, which then alarms our mind to prompt us to do whatever we need to do to survive (usually run).

Take a moment

Let me give you an example of how our minds love to have something to do. Right now, I just want you to observe your breath. I'll wait a minute while you do this.

How long did it take before your mind spoke up with some problem-solving chatter? 'Am I doing this right?' 'Should I be breathing more slowly?' 'Or more quickly?' 'Am I supposed to be counting my breaths?' 'This is a long minute!' 'What's the point of this?'

You didn't ask your mind to do anything, yet it offered an entire suite of options for you to choose from. 'Hi! I'm here! Please give me a job to do!' Interesting little things our minds, aren't they?

No problems

Our mind's problem-solving skills are always looking for a problem – even when there's no problem to solve.

If you are working on a spreadsheet, or changing a car tyre, or putting your baby to sleep, or learning piano, your mind has plenty to focus on. However, if you are doing a 'mindless' task, something that you can do on autopilot, like driving, or showering, or doing the washing up, your mind doesn't have to work hard, which is where the trouble starts. Minds struggle when they are asked to simply *be*. Instead, they seek their own gainful employment by inventing problems. We have evolved to listen to our minds like they speak the whole truth all the time, but minds can be a little prone to melodrama, and occasionally create a picture of reality that's not entirely accurate.

My story

My dog broke into the neighbours' yard a few months back. Henry has a strong prey drive and saw their chickens as fair game. I didn't know there was a hole in the fence and when he returned, he had a feather on his lip and there were no chickens in sight. I was panic-stricken and on the verge of tears, horrified at the poor chickens meeting their end at the paws of my dog.

The neighbours returned home and knocked on our door. When I opened the door, they jovially asked how we were and if they could borrow our mower because theirs was broken. I asked about their chickens. They looked confused and said, 'The chickens are fine and safe in their coop!' Nothing untoward had occurred, but that hadn't stopped my mind from jumping to some horrendous conclusions based on the small amount of information it had access to at the time.

We don't respond to reality exactly as it is, moment by moment. We spend most of our time thinking about the past or the future. We haven't evolved to evaluate whether or not what our mind is saying is helpful and will take us in the direction of living rich and meaningful lives, right here and now. Instead, we walk around like puppets, controlled by a very enthusiastic chatterbox with a tendency to focus too much on the negative.

In other words, we've evolved to listen to our minds automatically. Mindlessly, really. And, as we already know, autopilot is a crucial feature of the habit cycle. Until we learn otherwise, our approach to what our mind is saying usually occurs on autopilot and repeats unchecked.

To create self-supporting habits to live your bigger, better life, we need to interrupt the pattern of mindlessness. We need to become aware of what our mind is saying without entering into a struggle with it, and without judgement. Then it becomes about learning how to evaluate whether or not your thoughts are helpful, and if they are *un*helpful, creating distance between you and your mind, so you can choose an effective behavioural response.

At this point, you might be thinking, 'But Beck, surely there's a way I can just get rid of the thoughts I don't want to have?' I wish there was! And I'm sure you don't need to look far into your social media scroll to find a tiny quote in a pretty square that implores you to 'just think positive'.

Just like our feelings, our thoughts are internal

experiences that are outside our direct control. Yes, we can influence them, but we can't necessarily control when the thought will show up, how long it will stick around, when it will disappear, and whether or not it will return.

Let me give you an example. Right now, I *don't* want you to think about a giraffe. Don't think about its cute little horns or the wrinkles on its knees or its gangly legs and long neck. Do whatever you have to do in your mind to make sure that a giraffe does not feature.

What happened? Is there a cute little giraffe dancing across the stage in your mind right now? I thought so. And if you were able to keep the giraffe away, consider how much energy that took from you, before it likely returned once your focus lapsed.

It's true that most clients arrive in my therapy office hoping that I will teach them the secret to being able to control their thoughts. And while they're often surprised when I don't have the secret they are looking for, the good news is that I have something that's infinitely more effective: a tool for responding effectively to the chatterbox in our heads.

We're going to talk about accepting unhelpful thoughts. If you're rolling your eyes and feeling just a little frustrated that we're talking about acceptance of discomfort again, I get it! But I promise you that allowing discomfort to be present has the very important job of conserving your energy. That way, you can spend it instead on taking action towards the ways of being that are aligned with who you want to become.

We're not going to try and delete the thoughts that are unhelpful. Instead, our goal is simply to make peace with your mind being there without spending your energy wrestling with it.

An essential thing to remember as you go through this: you are not your mind.

Imagine that you are the sky. The thoughts in your mind, consisting of words, images, memories and sounds, are like the weather, passing through the sky. You're the observer of what your mind is doing. You have the ability to step back and simply witness its chatter without getting caught up in it. You have a choice as to how you respond to the information that your mind gives you. You can fight with it, engaging in internal warfare. You can tolerate it, suffering its presence, like it's an aunt or uncle you detest but have to see at family get-togethers. Or you can completely accept its place as part of your whole self and choose not to engage with it when it's being unhelpful. You can choose to conserve your energy for the things you can control: taking values-directed actions.

If your mind is having the thought that, 'Even though I'm tired, I know I'll feel really good after I go to the gym,' this could be considered a helpful thought if one of your values is to be healthy and active, and you can buy into it all you want. Helpful actions will follow if you give this thought energy and attention.

But if your mind is saying, 'Oh, I'm so tired, I just can't be bothered to go to the gym. I'll go tomorrow,' and it said this yesterday, and the day before, and last week and last month, then this thought is not helping you to act in alignment with your best self. Acknowledge your mind for doing its job but focus your energy on taking self-supporting action.

Imagine that you're in a game of tug-of-war, and there's another person on the end of the rope. When you pull hard, what does the other person do? They also pull hard! The intensity of the war escalates as you both try to win the game. Now, if you drop the rope, what happens to the other person? They're probably going to fall over. You've now removed yourself from the war. The other person might still be holding the rope, jumping up and down, taunting you and trying to get you to re-engage in the contest, but if you've dropped the rope, you're no longer spending energy on the fight.

Getting unhooked

This is the approach to take with your mind. It will still be present, offering you thoughts that act as bait to attract your attention, inviting you into a struggle . . . but you don't need to bite.

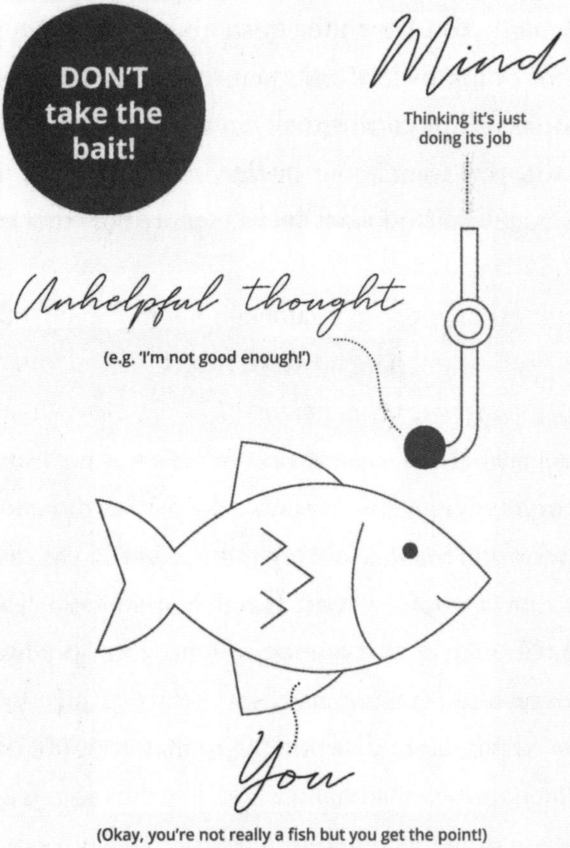

Don't put effort into trying to eliminate, ignore or suppress unhelpful thoughts, or try to change them into positive thoughts, because that would be engaging in the struggle. Instead, you spit the hook out and focus on your actions (and when you become practised at spitting the hook out, you'll be able to observe your unhelpful thoughts without taking the bait at all – just keep swimming!). You have the choice to acknowledge your mind for doing its job, and then to spend your mental, emotional and physical energy on taking action that fits with who you want to be in that moment. Let's jump off the page and into your life to explore how this looks.

Take a moment

Bring awareness to what your mind is saying. Is the thought helpful for moving you in the direction of who you want to be? If the answer is yes, the thought is helpful. Give it as much attention as you like. Go with it. If the answer is no, then practise acknowledging your mind for doing its job, and then unhooking yourself from that thought by letting it play in the background, like the radio is on but you're not listening to it closely. This is a great strategy for being able to recognise that your mind is there but making the choice not to get involved. Another unhooking technique is to thank your mind for doing its job. If your mind is saying, 'Oh, I'm so tired, I cannot be bothered to go to the gym,' you could respond with, 'Thanks, mind. Thank you. Thank you for giving me that thought and doing your job to keep me safe from discomfort. But, right now, this is not a good use of my time and energy, so I'm going to let that thought be and go about my day.'

See how this approach gives you a little distance from your mind? It helps you to disengage from getting caught up in the thought, to simply observing the thought and taking action anyway. If your mind regularly thinks in image form, I invite you to try unhooking from those pictures by imagining they are part of a dramatic movie trailer version of your (usually past or future) experience that your mind is playing you. Let it play in the background, but don't jump into the movie.

Once you've acknowledged your mind, come back to your breath. Take a couple of slow and steady full breaths. This helps to ground your nervous system and undo any physical responses that have occurred in reply to the unhelpful thoughts. Then choose which actions you could take right now that are consistent with the bigger, better life you're out to create. Practice really helps you to remember that you've got this technique in your toolbox to change your experience.

MANAGING UNHELPFUL THOUGHTS

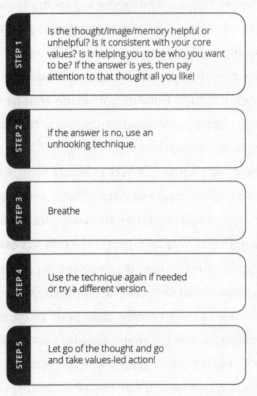

STEP 1 Is the thought/image/memory helpful or unhelpful? Is it consistent with your core values? Is it helping you to be who you want to be? If the answer is yes, then pay attention to that thought all you like!

STEP 2 If the answer is no, use an unhooking technique.

STEP 3 Breathe

STEP 4 Use the technique again if needed or try a different version.

STEP 5 Let go of the thought and go and take values-led action!

If your mind is telling you that this won't work, remember how clever minds are at doing their jobs. You're attempting to do something new, that requires some effort to learn and practise, and your mind wants to protect you from that because it sounds hard. They try to keep us in the cycle of self-sabotage, because it feels familiar and safe and more comfortable than doing something differently. When this happens, use your awareness and unhooking techniques on the 'It won't work' thought. Say to your mind, 'Thank you for giving me this thought. I know you want to keep me comfortable. But I'm not giving that thought energy right now. Instead, I'm going to take action in line with my values.'

Practise as often as you possibly can. Initially, you might like to practise in a quiet, uninterrupted way. Then, as you become more comfortable with responding to your thoughts with mindful detachment and awareness, you can incorporate this technique as you're going about your daily life.

Sometimes, unhelpful thoughts become so ingrained in our internal dialogue that it can be difficult to find the language to change the conversation. If you regularly notice self-critical thoughts, you may recognise the list below. Practise the self-encouragement statements instead to help you develop a kinder inner voice.

SELF-ENCOURAGEMENT

SELF-SUPPORTING RESPONSE

- I gave it my best shot, today.
- I did ____________________ well, today.
- I'm on the right path for me.
- My healing work is brave work.
- I'm scared because I care.
- I believe in my capabilities.
- I showed up today.
- I've got this.
- I don't judge myself for messing up.
  I celebrate myself for putting it back together.

SELF-CRITICAL RESPONSE

- I'm a failure.
- I never get anything right.
- If I was smart, I would know where I was headed.
- I'm broken.
- I'm scared because I'm weak.
- I can't do it.
- I'm a mess.
- There's no point in trying.
- Everyone else has their life together.
  I'm a loser because I have problems.

Inner acceptance

Your thoughts and feelings occur almost simultaneously and are often accompanied by bodily sensations as well. So, while we've explored how to respond to thoughts and feelings individually, we can't realistically separate our internal world into mutually exclusive categories. We accept uncomfortable feelings while accepting unhelpful thoughts, and vice versa. How can you respond mindfully to your thoughts and feelings at the same time?

My story

I want to tell you another story about my dog, Henry, my Weimaraner. At five months old, he developed a tumour on his hip and surgery was required to assess whether or not the tumour was malignant.

While my highest values centre on the commitment I have to the people and animals that I love, I knew on this particular day that sitting in the vet's reception area, waiting for the surgery to be over, was not going to help me to help Henry, and would likely not help the vet either. In prioritising my values, those I love come first. There was nothing more I could do.

The values that followed on this particular day were my capacity to make a difference in the lives of my clients. Henry's surgery was on a day when I was scheduled to be working at my practice, so I went to work. I knew that I had the psychological strategies to cope emotionally and support my clients effectively.

In supporting my clients, talking through their own pain and whatever was showing up for them in their sessions that day, can you imagine what my mind was doing? Probably something along the lines of, 'Is he going to be okay? Am I going to lose him? Is it going to be cancer?'. Can you imagine what I was feeling? And what would have happened to the intensity of these thoughts and feelings if I had tried to make them go away? They would have been magnified.

Instead, I used acceptance. As I was seeing my clients, I was also holding space for my anxiety by describing the feeling to myself. I recall it showed up as a blue cloud of anxiety in my chest.

Using these techniques while I was working, I was sitting there listening to my clients, helping them through their own stuff, and at the same time, breathing into and around the anxiety I was experiencing to make room for it to be present. I was also silently responding to my mind's concerns with, 'Thanks, mind, thank you for doing your job and warning me of what could go wrong. But focusing on those thoughts is not a good use of time and energy right now.'

This was an exercise of inner acceptance. I accepted feeling uncomfortable because I cared. I accepted feeling uncomfortable because this mattered to me deeply. I love Henry like he's my child (as I write this, he's 12, so the outcome of this story is a happy one!), and while I care about my dog, I am also incredibly committed to my clients.

We often exist in the space of duality. We can feel uncomfortable, but we can still live by our values at the same time. This is an example of how we respond to our internal experiences as they occur in our daily lives.

Practise the acceptance techniques for feelings and thoughts. Observe your internal experiences, and completely accept them as part of the wholeness of your present moment. Use the techniques to accept the discomfort while committing to taking values-directed action to build your bigger life.

Remember: these habits you're learning are not abstract concepts to be left on a shelf! They are practical exercises to help you to manage your thoughts and feelings as you go about living your life.

Case study: Mira

When Mira started managing her time in a way that was aligned with her values, she came up against unhelpful thoughts that felt strong enough to roadblock her progress. Thoughts like, 'I don't have time for this', 'I must check my phone and emails in case there is something urgent that I'm missing', 'I'll just deal with this one thing and then I'll go back to time-blocking', and 'This is too hard', were loud and insistent in her mind, often convincing her that they were the truth. It took a few weeks of consistent practice for Mira to confidently detach from these thoughts. Of course, the process continues to be imperfect, as it is for all of us, but she is now able to stick to her values-based scheduling even when her mind tries to convince her that it knows best!

Take a moment

In earlier chapters, we spoke about the importance of going gently through the change process. I want to support you to do that with your mind by practising speaking to yourself with compassion. Although it might feel artificial at first, practising these compassionate self-statements daily helps reshape your relationship with yourself by changing your internal conversation.

Compassionate self-statements

- ☐ I am trying as hard as I can.
- ☐ I acknowledge myself for showing up.
- ☐ I'm not broken, I'm learning new ways of doing things.
- ☐ I am deserving of the time and effort to make this change for myself.
- ☐ I'm allowed to start again, no matter how many times it takes.
- ☐ I give myself permission to be human!
- ☐ Everyone feels anxious at times, and this is really hard for me.
- ☐ My discomfort is normal, and I can still give it a go.

- ☐ I am not alone in experiencing hard times.
- ☐ I'm doing a great job despite everything I'm facing right now.
- ☐ I give myself permission to rest when I need to.

Add yours here:

....

....

....

....

....

....

....

....

....

....

....

....

....

....

....

....

....

....

....

9

Support crew

One of the pivotal elements to letting go of habits of self-sabotage and becoming who you want to be is having a support crew around you. The people who hold space for you as you dismantle the habits that are no longer workable in your life and create new habits that are self-supporting will be crucial to the change process itself.

Count on yourself

First of all, it's essential to acknowledge that the person you need most is *you*. As you adopt a new way of being in whatever area of your life you want to make adjustments to, your identity will change. In fact, your identity *has* to change for the new habits to be securely woven into your future. As you build trust in yourself to take actions in line with your values rather than actions that push you further away from where you want to be, you will see yourself differently. You will come to know yourself as someone who does what they say they are going to do.

This might initially feel foreign for you. You might find that you have spent so long doubting yourself and being convinced that you are someone who doesn't follow through that this place of self-trust might feel a little shaky, at least to begin with. You can expect that the change you're making will re-establish your entire relationship with yourself. You're going to meet yourself anew: a person you can trust to follow through, keep promises, and show up. A person you can count on, even when it gets hard. A person you can rely on to take action today that your future self will thank you for.

Take a moment

Reflect on who you want to be: the best version of yourself. Sometimes, thinking about your values might not be enough to anchor you. When your present self is deep in self-sabotage, it can be difficult to keep sight of what's important. In this place, we struggle to find perspective and impulsively continue to reach for comfort. In these times, turn to your future self for guidance. Imagine your wise and calm older self. Who is that person? What do they stand for? What would make them proud of you, right now?

This is who you're creating: the best version of yourself.

In doing so, you let go of your old identity. For example, if you see yourself as someone who never completes what they set out to do, you're more likely to leave your assignments to the last minute or give up on the course you've just started. Your dream business will remain a set of scribbled ideas on the back of a napkin. You'll abandon learning to paint when you don't get it perfect on the first go. All because this is the identity that you're living into.

As you build your bigger life, the more action you take in alignment with your values, the more evidence your brain has that this is who you are now. Every choice you make to move closer to connect with your best self is concrete evidence that your brain uses to rewire neural pathways to mark your self-supporting habits as worth repeating. And with practice, this is how these new habits take over your habits of self-sabotage. This evidence becomes confidence and self-belief, and eventually, your sense of identity changes with it.

Every step in the right direction counts. Even when you trip up. Even when you go backwards for a while. As long as you come back to the path, you're progressing. And that's why you are the most important person throughout this entire journey.

Count on your change community

But like I said, you don't have to do this alone. In fact, I don't recommend trying to change your habits on your own. Having a change community around you will make the process easier, and help you stick to it for longer. It's worth finding your people when we're talking about something as important as transforming your life!

When it comes to changing an unhelpful habit, it's often more easily done as part of a group. Sharing challenges, frustrations, slip-ups, fears, doubts and the general discomfort of doing life differently to what you usually do is easier when you can see others going through the same experiences and challenges. Seeing someone you identify with make the change you want to make provides a sense of hope. 'If she can do it, I must be able to do it, too.'

This is the beauty of groups of people seeking to make the same change. It provides evidence for your brain about the possibility of change being real before you might have created the evidence with your own actions. And there are different styles of groups – groups that you may attend in person and be intimately involved in, or groups that you might be part of online where your participation is more passive, but there is still that same capacity to be inspired.

You don't have to join a group, though. You can create your own change community. I would recommend that the change community that you create for yourself includes the following people:

- an accountability person
- an encouragement person
- people who are on the same path to making change as you are.

An accountability person or buddy is someone who helps you honour your commitment to yourself. This is the person who will challenge you on your excuses and blocks that will show up along the way (because I promise you that excuses and blocks always show up – for all of us!). An accountability person is someone who can see the big picture of the change you're making and keep in mind where you're headed. This is especially useful when you're stuck in the middle of change and can no longer see the start line, but you can't yet see the finish line either.

An accountability person is most effective when they are someone you respect and admire. You need someone who you will take seriously in this role to ensure you'll listen to them when they call you out on your stuff!

Your accountability person is likely to be different to the person who provides you with emotional support and encouragement. The reason for this is that their role is to keep you on the path, even when they need to say things that are hard for you to hear but help you get out of your own way.

My story

When I was writing my second book, *The Universe Listens to Brave*, I was not in a great place to be writing with ease and flow. At the time, I had a four-month-old baby who was experiencing a significant sleep regression and waking seven times a night. I was sleep-deprived, emotional, and had great difficulty seeing a way through it all to deliver my manuscript to my publisher on time. I was in a place where my doubt around my capacity to write threatened to sabotage the entire book. I messaged my friend, Dave. I think the exact wording of my message was something along the lines of, 'This is so hard, Dave. Tell me something that will make me write this book.' Now, Dave is not the friend I go to when I want a virtual hug. He's not the friend I go to when I just want someone to lament with me that sometimes life sucks. Dave's strengths are his logical thinking patterns and his blunt communication style, wrapped up in the fact that I know he believes in me and has my best interests at heart. He responded shortly after I sent my message with, 'Beck, deadlines don't care about feelings.' Harsh, but true, and that was exactly why I went to Dave – because I needed a reality check that wasn't wrapped up in cotton wool.

He became my accountability person for that book, and I messaged him every time I completed a chapter. He cheered me on and reminded me that I could do it, but not before he gave me a hard but heart-filled truth. I think it's important to note here that Dave and I have a friendship that spans years. We know each other very well and our friendship is founded in respect and mutual admiration. Without that basis, it's possible I wouldn't take his feedback as seriously as I do. And I want the same for you. Make sure your accountability person is someone who gets you and can communicate to you in a way that will make their message clear to you without it possibly meaning something else, especially something about your worth or your capacity to move forward in the direction that you want to go.

Your encouragement person or buddy is the person who provides you with emotional support. They remind you to bring compassion to yourself and they remind you of what you're capable of. This is the person who reminds you to give yourself credit for the steps you're making in the right direction, and for how far you've come. Your encouragement person is your cheerleader.

External feedback from your encouragement person

can play a vital role in giving you this evidence, especially because in the initial stages, others can often see the changes in us better than we can. This is particularly important if you're the type of person who can become fixated on the finish line, or impatient with your results.

The change doesn't have to be made by you alone and there may be some parts of the path that you can't do without a little extra assistance. Consider if there is other expertise or professional guidance that you may also need to let go of your habits of self-sabotage? Asking for help for a behavioural rut in which you find yourself stuck is a way of honouring yourself and committing to change because, sometimes, it's impossible to find the way out by ourselves.

Take a moment

My change community

My accountability person:

....

....

....

My encouragement person:

....

....

....

Professional help/expertise I may need:

....

....

....

Groups to join:

....

....

....

When change challenges others

As you embark on this journey to create new habits for a bigger life, the reality is that not everyone will be supportive of the changes you're trying to make. Some people will be threatened by your growth because it holds up a mirror in which they are forced to look at themselves. Those that are threatened are the ones who don't want to see where they are also stuck. Some people will refuse to support your growth, or even act to sabotage it, because they are invested in the present version of you – the one that makes them feel comfortable with where they are also at in life.

Erin's story

Erin explained to me that she'd done a significant amount of work on herself in the past couple of years. By 'work', she clarified that she had changed the way she thought about herself, changed her relationship with her body, and let go of many beliefs which were previously keeping her stuck. She'd challenged herself personally and professionally. And she was somewhat taken aback when what she saw as valuable personal growth had unexpectedly left her feeling disconnected from friends with whom she had been very close for a long time.

She was saddened at the thought that her hard-won transformation – her own grit, determination and dreams – were now resulting in people she cared for shifting further away from her because she'd 'changed'. They were the ones who were usually by her side through it all. Now it seemed like they were distracted at best and, at worst, unavailable. Erin was a new version of herself and some friendships were not in a place to accept this. Those friendships reached their natural conclusion as Erin grew in a different direction. Other friendships strengthened in celebration of that growth.

Personal evolution is not predictable. For some people, it happens only as a side effect of ageing and it may not be recognised or celebrated. For others, it's front and centre on their priority list. People who value personal growth deliberately seek out lessons from change and rise to the challenge when it arrives, actively shaping themselves on each path they take.

Our lives exist within a social system (family, friends, colleagues – anyone that plays a role in our lives long-term). Each person in our social system is also on their own path, participating in their own lives while also responding to what life gives them. Each of our lives is dynamic.

Our social system generally includes friends who have similar values to our own. It's sharing the things that are important to us that make us feel connected.

A complementary value system is the fabric of a friendship that has you feeling like Jane really 'gets' you.

And when it comes to family, we are usually raised to have values that reflect those of our parents or caregivers. It's worth noting that sometimes, people have parents who practise values that they actively avoid as adults. There is a saying that goes, 'You can pick your friends but not your family', and it perfectly epitomises the adults for whom family was an example of what not to do.

Where am I going with this? I'm saying that we form long-term bonds with people because the things we hold dear, and the way we approach the world, are similar. They are the group to which we belong because we share the same values.

The thing we often forget is that we are all growing over time, some of us consciously and purposefully, like Erin, and others not so obviously. Each of us is out there living our lives in a way that works for us at the time. If you and your friends have been alongside each other for years, then it follows that occasionally change will make it tough to stay together. We can get out of alignment. We evolve at different rates. Life may happen and change course for us. And at the end of the day, we may be left feeling separated from the ones who had once been an influential presence on our path.

This was the case for Erin. After letting go of her self-sabotaging habits to begin creating habits that were aligned with her best self, she felt separate from her people. Disconnected. Different, even. And the thing is, she *is* different within herself. Her discomfort was around the fact that she felt unrecognisable to the people who were once close friends. While no one had done anything to hurt anyone else in her friendship group, Erin's personal growth had meant some friends had grown apart and now had different values.

At this point, I wish I could present a piece of binding magic, the powers of which would return people to each other. But, of course, it's not that easy. In the absence of magical powers, here are some things to consider for your journey and those of the people around you.

Sometimes, growth is so personal that it needs to be done alone. That means that you may not wish to share your goals with everyone, or anyone, for that matter. Parts of your change journey might hurt. Important growth is like that. And some people cope better with pain if they have space to process it before they share it. Distance like this is often temporary. Remember, it's not just you that needs space through some chapters – your people might need that space, too.

Just because you feel like a new and improved version

of yourself doesn't mean every person around you will see you like that. Some people might be threatened by your transformation. Growth can be uncomfortable for some because it confronts them with what's not working in their own lives. This kind of confrontation can fracture a friendship or relationship when someone grows at a pace that the other person is not yet ready for. Expecting others to always *get it* when no two people ever walk exactly the same life path will leave you with a case of the disses: disappointed, dissatisfied and disconnected.

We all want to be understood. We want to be seen and heard, because sharing ourselves helps to make sense of our own journey. But it's worth remembering that sometimes the only one who can understand your journey is you. Mind your expectations.

Sometimes, feeling disconnected is a sign that we need to work harder to reconnect. Perhaps it's information that you have been a little absent in the friendship or relationship, or that your friend may also be feeling distant. Do you need to work harder? Does the friendship need more of you in some way?

On the other hand, if this feeling has been happening for a while, perhaps it's a sign that you no longer share similar values and have grown apart. Not all relationships, whether they be family, friends or lovers, are meant to last our entire lifetime. Do you need to let go? Do you need a different community around you that fits the change you're making?

The truth is, no one needs to understand your journey but you. Seeking validation from others may undermine the inherent value in your evolution. Celebrate your own transformation. You know how far you've come.

Choose your support crew mindfully and remember that you don't have to do this all alone. Choose who you share your transformation with, based on who you trust to have your back. The change process is a time of incredible vulnerability. We are easily shaken in the early weeks (maybe even months) and risk a return to old habits. Don't allow anyone alongside you who will create more instability. If someone close to you is not supportive of the change you're making, compensate for their lack of support by seeking the company, encouragement and comradeship of others who *do* support and understand where you're at and where you're headed.

Here's to connection with ourselves and with our people. And here's to having the respect for ourselves and for our people to evolve without judgement and with gentle, accepting expectations.

Case study: Mira

Mira had been relying on her wife to be her 'everything'. Her wife was her accountability person, encouragement person and her 'community', in that she also wanted to make a similar change (Mira's wife was similarly invested in having more balance across her values and organisation in her schedule). While I fully support such a close connection between partners, problems can arise if we expect our partner to be the source and solution for all our needs. In Mira's case, her wife was working long hours outside the home, so she wasn't available to provide Mira with encouragement in a timely manner throughout the day. The other obstacle they faced is that Mira didn't really take her wife seriously as an accountability person – which isn't surprising considering it's our partners who see us at our best and our *worst*! Mira set about assembling a support crew outside her relationship. A friend who had started on a fitness regimen acted as an accountability partner, and Mira served in the same role for her friend. A supervisor from Mira's previous job became her encouragement person, and Mira joined a

Facebook group that shared tips and hacks for productivity to access ongoing inspiration from people who were also working on scheduling their time according to their values.

10

Getting back when you've gone off track

The routines that we set up for our days are essential because what we do by habit accounts for 40–45 per cent of our actions. Aligning your daily routines with your values will result in improving the quality of your entire life. The more you have ritualised in your life, the more willpower you'll have remaining to devote to demanding tasks. And the more demanding things you're able to do in your life, the wider your comfort zone grows. Life becomes braver and more meaningful.

When it comes to changing habits of self-sabotage, we interrupt the self-defeating cycle with awareness. We make a choice to respond to the cue differently. But as with anything worthwhile, the honeymoon phase of dopamine-induced motivation wears off and things inevitably become harder before they get easier. And then . . . we get off track.

Creating small habits to build a bigger life is never going to happen in a straight line. We improve our habits along the way, often through trial and error. This is not because you're doing it incorrectly, or because there's something defective within you – it's because you're human. That's why one of the most important topics we can ever discuss when it comes to changing habits is what to do when you get off track.

We increase our self-knowledge by constantly reviewing our new routines to see if they work. Sometimes, the only way we can know if something is going to be effective for us in the long-term is to try it out and then review how effective it is. The more often you stop to review the changes you're making, the quicker you'll be able to course-correct when needed.

Failing forward

It is so important that you give yourself permission to fail and start again – as many times as it takes. This is how all change occurs. We continually make course corrections to come closer to alignment with our values. And when we get off track, we return to our values as the foundation and purpose for the change.

My story

I did a walking challenge for charity, committing to walk 13 kilometres every day for 30 days. While I had no intention of walking 13 kilometres every single day as a lifetime habit, this challenge served as a pattern interrupt following a long period of being disconnected from my body due to a traumatic pregnancy. I was introducing movement again (albeit in a big way!). I surprised myself for the first couple of weeks. It was tough, but I was impressed that I got up every day and did the walk. Announcing it on social media helped for my accountability.

On day 17, I injured my ankle. A set of muscles in my ankle became stressed from the repetitive strain and I had to seek treatment from a physiotherapist, who instructed me to take a few rest days. This was not part of my plan. The interruption to my goal was annoying and threatened to derail me completely. My physio then advised me to split the walk up so that I wasn't walking more than 8 kilometres at a time. This required me to walk 8 kilometres in the morning, ice my ankle a few times during the day, and then complete the remaining 5 kilometres in the afternoon. The disruption that the injury caused was almost enough for me to abandon the challenge entirely. It took so much extra energy for me to complete two walks per day. It felt like I was doubling the willpower required because I had to start twice a day. If it wasn't for the fact that I'd announced the challenge on social media, I don't think I would have continued.

New habits are really vulnerable. They're vulnerable when stress shows up and when life gets in the way. Once the habit is disrupted, your brain immediately encourages you to return to what's familiar and comfortable, which is your self-defeating – but relief-providing – habit.

In research on quitting smoking, participants generally gave up smoking and then relapsed as soon as a stressful event occurred. This happened on the first one to three attempts at quitting. By the fourth attempt to quit, people began to predict that they'd have the urge to smoke when stress showed up. By this stage, they would take this a step further by planning alternatives to smoking for coping with anticipated stress. By attempt number seven, the rate of relapse was significantly lower, and many people are able to give up smoking completely.

This is all to say that it is essential to approach the change process with realistic expectations and compassion for your human and imperfect self. If you plan to fail and prepare a contingency plan accordingly, then your recovery becomes faster and, eventually, the habit will change permanently.

The prison of perfectionism

If you identify as someone who leans towards perfectionism, please go gently on yourself. Perfectionism can bring limiting beliefs that act as roadblocks to the change process.

Perfectionism is born of fear. It is the misguided belief that if you can achieve perfection, you can avoid the pain of failure, judgement or humiliation. The problem is that perfection is simply impossible when it comes to being human. Perfectionism also increases our need for control.

Seeking control feels like an antidote to anxiety, especially the anxiety that shows up around making change. We want a guarantee that our efforts will work and will be worth it. But all perfectionism does is tightens anxiety's grip on you, creating a mouse-wheel of attempts to control everything that could result in imperfection. Here, we meet head-on with all the uncontrollables: other people, our personal resources (time, money, motivation, emotional, physical and cognitive energy), our internal experiences with thoughts and feelings, the past, and the future. We run and run on the impossible mouse-wheel of control until we burn out and hit peak emotional exhaustion. The rational side of you understands that you can't control everything and perfection is impossible, but the emotional side of you has no other way to reckon with fear. The result is paralysis.

There is another way that will save your sanity, energy and emotional wellbeing – and that is to release your grip throughout the process of changing your habits by remembering that:

- Fear is out to protect you, but its stories about future-based dilemmas are usually far more melodramatic than any reality we live into.
- We live under the illusion of control. Actually, we survive perfectly well (pardon the

perfectionism pun) controlling far less than we like to believe we do.

- Emotional discomfort is a fact of life. While we can't avoid it, we can choose discomfort for growth and living bravely and meaningfully rather than discomfort of stagnation, hiding from life, and masking our true selves.
- There is no such thing as perfection. Giving yourself permission to stop striving and, instead, simply showing up as best as you can today is where freedom starts.
- Your future self will always be more grateful for the results of you taking action than looking back on time wasted in a state of fear-induced paralysis.

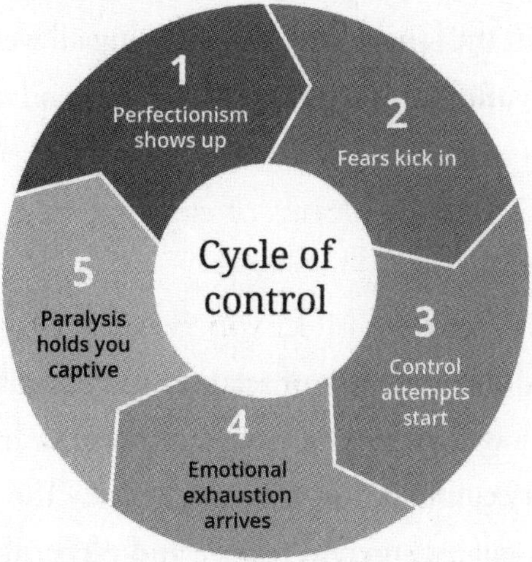

And as you create new habits for a better life, applying such rigid expectations and standards to your transformation is only going to create deeper pain when you slip up. That's right, I intentionally said when, and not if, because for the vast majority of us, slipping up is an essential part of the journey. Our recovery from these blips determines how enduring our new set of habits and our new psychological landscape will be.

Failing is not only normal, it's to be expected. Your success in overcoming self-sabotage will come more readily when you anticipate getting off track and plan for how you'll get back on track. Research has shown that allowing ourselves to relapse in a small way improves the chances of long-term success. For example, one small bowl of ice cream when you feel like it during the week is more workable in the long-term than bingeing all weekend. Go gently on your path – your best self is depending on it!

Relapse

There are different stages of relapse, and identifying these different stages means you can catch a slide off track before it becomes a full-blown setback. The stages are emotional relapse, mental relapse and physical relapse.

At the **emotional relapse** stage, you're not consciously thinking about self-sabotage, but your emotions and actions may be setting you up for relapse in the near future. For example, you might be tired, and you might have had a series of hard days this week, and you've skipped a couple of days of your new routine.

Mental relapse is the next stage. This occurs when there's warfare happening in your mind. The version of yourself who wants to stay on track is fighting with your fragile self who's lobbying to return to self-sabotage. This is when you have an awareness that part of you wants to give in and return to your self-defeating (but comfortable and familiar) habits, and part of you wants to stay on track to developing new, self-supporting habits.

And finally, the last stage is **physical relapse**. This is when you are actively engaging in your old habits. Self-sabotage re-occurs and you're off track, doing the things you don't want to be doing, but which give you short-term relief from the mental and physical effort of sticking to your new habits.

But the thing is, it's never as simple as saying to yourself, 'Just start again!' It's important to acknowledge the suffering we endure when we get off track. It's a painful process. The emotional, mental and practical fallout might include loss of self-trust, feelings of unworthiness, helplessness, hopelessness, frustration, overwhelm, anger, sadness, embarrassment and shame. You may question your sense of identity, for example, 'Maybe I'm someone who will never follow through to get my health in check.' You might experience increased self-criticism and you might find yourself self-sabotaging for longer and to a greater extent as a form of self-punishment.

Progress through self-compassion

Let's look at this cycle. You're in the process of adopting a new habit that's aligned with who you want to be. You go well for a couple of days, and then some kind of stress shows up in your life. You procrastinate to avoid facing the discomfort, or you ditch your new routine in favour of returning to your old routine because it's more comfortable. Then you feel guilty for not doing the new habit in the way that you promised yourself that you would. This makes you feel worse, so you eat or drink or medicate or spend to numb your feelings of guilt. You then criticise yourself for being out of alignment and beat up on yourself for getting off track. This makes you feel even worse, so you repeat your self-sabotage actions in an attempt to get some relief.

Do you see how this cycle digs the hole even deeper?

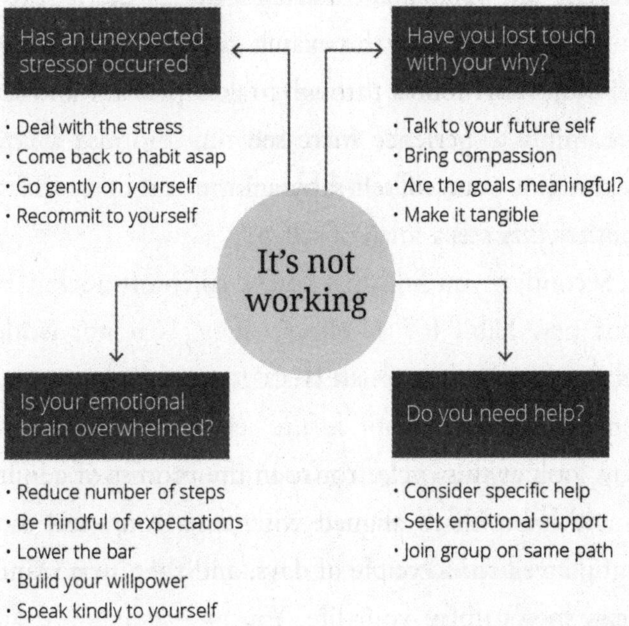

Here is another approach to regrouping after a slip-up. This will allow you to continue moving forward rather than lapsing into a pattern of self-criticism followed by more self-sabotage.

First, bring compassion and acceptance to yourself. You are human, not a robot. Be mindful of the urge to punish yourself. No amount of punishment will bring you back on track and keep you there. Instead, it's likely to push you further into self-sabotage. The more you disconnect from yourself and buy into the belief that you're not good enough and/or unable to change, the harder it is to get back on track. Speak to yourself kindly. Remember that building new neural pathways takes practice and time. Recommit to yourself with one tiny promise followed by one tiny step, followed by another tiny promise, and another tiny step.

Second, if you find that you've fallen off track, review your new habit for its effectiveness. Is it not working because you've lost touch with your why? If so, have a conversation with your future self and reconnect with why this new way of being is so important to you. Check in with yourself to evaluate if your goals are still meaningful and remind yourself of what it is that you're out to create in your life.

Is it not working because you need help? Consider if you've stopped making progress because you can't do this alone. Consider the specific help that you need. Perhaps there's solutions available, but you don't have the skillset or knowledge to implement them. Asking for help is an excellent and very effective problem-solving strategy.

Perhaps it's not working because you don't have adequate emotional support available to you. Sometimes, the difference between success and failure of new habits is just having the presence of someone who's got our back. Join a group on the same path for maintaining inspiration and encouragement. One of the most helpful things is to simply be reminded that you're not the only one that really has to rally in times of things getting hard.

Is it not working because you're feeling overwhelmed? In this case, reduce the number of steps that you are asking yourself to do. Break the habit down into smaller parts and conquer the initial part of the habit first before adding more steps.

Habit change results in identity change, and it changes our relationship with ourselves for the better. Because you will get off track at some point in the process, we also need to note that there is a line between being compassionate with yourself and allowing yourself to cop out and give up. I call this radical responsibility.

> **Radical responsibility is about recognising that if nothing changes, nothing changes. And nothing changes if we don't acknowledge our role in keeping ourselves stuck. Nothing changes if we don't acknowledge the effort needed to create change. Nothing changes if we refuse to accept the discomfort of change.**

Nothing changes if we pretend we're not sliding off track. And nothing changes if we stay in denial, hoping someone else will do the work for us.

Take a moment

Have you ever heard of the saying, 'Give an inch, take a mile'? Bringing compassion to our efforts to change self-sabotage habits also requires that we learn where the line is to pull ourselves up. Without knowing where this line is, we can end up going too gently and allowing ourselves to unravel into even more self-sabotage. In doing so, we create an inner audit for accountability and encouragement.

To step into radical responsibility, set aside judgement and readiness to dispense punishment and ask yourself the following questions from a place of curiosity and self-enquiry. These questions help us to maintain the standards we set for ourselves, but they are not tools for condemning ourselves based on our mistakes, relapses or fragilities.

- ☐ Have I tried as hard as I could have?
- ☐ Did I put aside the time to plan properly?
- ☐ Did I seek help when it became apparent that I couldn't do it all myself?
- ☐ Did I use the resources I had available to me?
- ☐ Did I review my goal and make course corrections as needed?
- ☐ Did I take actions that I am proud of?
- ☐ Did I take actions that were in alignment with my values?
- ☐ Did I set up my environment to maximise my chances of doing the things I wanted to do?
- ☐ Did I set up my environment to minimise my chances of doing the things I didn't want to do?
- ☐ Did I take care of myself in a way that replenished my cognitive resources?
- ☐ Did I give myself credit for the effort I've been making?
- ☐ Did I speak to myself respectfully and kindly?
- ☐ Did I consult with my future self?

Your answers to these questions will show you what adjustments you can make to your new habits moving forward, so that they are more likely to stick.

Self-trust

One of the essential elements of any change process is the cultivation of self-trust. The process of building trust starts with making one tiny promise to yourself and keeping it, over and over again. When we talk about creating small habits to build a bigger, better life, we are always talking about, 'How do I trust myself to do the things I say I will do?'

When self-defeating behaviours reach a point where they have significantly disrupted our alignment with our values, they erode self-trust. Our sense of worthiness becomes fragile. We use self-sabotage as 'evidence' of the negative beliefs we have developed about ourselves based on our unworkable actions. The result is a lack of self-belief and a deep conviction that we're unable to change.

To come back to a place of self-trust, start by showing up for yourself through values-directed action. Make one tiny promise to yourself. Keep that tiny promise to yourself. You now have one tiny piece of evidence that you are very capable of showing up for yourself. Then repeat this over and over again. It's a promise that is kept emotionally, mentally and, especially, physically. As we relearn to trust ourselves, our relationship with ourselves strengthens.

We don't always have to build evidence from scratch, though. You can use the evidence you already have from times in the past when you have shown up for yourself. Think about one of those times now. What did you do? How did you feel? If you let go of judgement, attack and self-criticism, what do you already know about yourself and your past actions that proves you *can* show up for yourself?

Use gratitude as medicine for continuing on your path. An essential part of showing up for ourselves is to bring gratitude to the process. Thank yourself for how hard you're trying right now. Thank yourself for how hard you've tried in the past. Thank your future self for having faith in you. Acknowledge everything that you're currently doing, especially when it's darn hard!

Keep in mind that the longer you're off track, the more likely you are to feel lost. Slipping up and falling back into old habits can bring up feelings of uncertainty. You might feel unsure of where you're headed, except around the avoidance roundabout. You might feel unsure of what to do to catch yourself, or unsure of who you are, unsure of whether you'll ever get unstuck, unsure of who you can trust, including yourself, and unsure of what's really important. These are the feelings of disconnection. You're not actually lost, you've just become separated from your best self. The process can happen insidiously, or quickly in one big 'blowout'. It can also happen through simple forgetfulness, because new habits take cognitive effort and old habits are automatic, leading us to do them without thinking.

If you're in this place, remind yourself of what the change will bring you and why it's important. Remind yourself of how the actions you're taking are making your values tangible through lived experience. Tell your change community about your commitment to yourself and ask for help if you need it.

Long-term habit change takes time. And because you're not a robot, there will come a time when you'll need a break. There is a difference between taking a break and self-sabotage. Taking a break doesn't mean you're giving up or copping out. Brains need time to decompress. If your nerves feel frayed, or life presents a twist that demands more resources than you have, then rest is necessary – if not essential – for now. Change needs periods of rest so that your brain has a chance to catch up with your new way of being. This doesn't mean that you give up putting effort into changing. It means that change doesn't receive all your energy in that moment.

When you're off track, you might struggle to identify when to start again. The good news is there is no bad time to start again. You can start again as soon as you become aware of being off track. You can start again when you realise you're copping out. You can start again when you're finished wallowing – and as an Olympic-level tantrum thrower, I get what it's like to navigate the emotions of not doing the things you say you'll do! You can start again when you realise the power is in your hands. You can start again when you've gotten off track for the 49th or the 99th time. You can start again when someone re-inspires you or whenever something shows up that encourages you.

There's no bad time to start again.

Case study: Mira

Mira had some initial teething problems with her new schedule. She had allocated less time than needed for some tasks, and too much time for others. A few adjustments and her schedule felt manageable . . . until her wife injured her back and was home from work for two weeks while she recovered. Mira didn't just feel that she fell off track during this time. She felt like all her efforts to create a sustainable work/life rhythm went out the window as she helped care for her wife. She fell back into old habits of loading up her to-do list and then decompensating into a sense of urgency and overwhelm. By the time her wife returned to work, Mira felt like she was starting all over again. In fact, she wasn't starting again, because the changes she had been working on counted towards new neural pathways for work/life rhythm. While willpower was still required to recommence time-blocking according to her values, once she did, Mira picked it up again more quickly than before.

Take a moment

Self-trust evidence

When have you shown up for yourself in the past?

....

....

....

What did you do?

....

....

....

How did you feel?

....

....

....

If you let go of judgement, attack and self-criticism, what do you already know about yourself and your past actions that proves you can show up for yourself?

....

....

....

....

....

....

....

....

....

....

....

....

....

....

....

....

My contingency plan

When I notice emotional relapse, I'll take these steps:

....

....

....

When I notice mental relapse, I'll take these steps:

....

....

....

When I notice physical relapse, I'll take these steps:

....

....

....

These are the things I'll say to myself to offer myself compassion:

....

....

....

Small affirmations for a big life

I want to leave you with my reminders for change-makers. These are affirmations you can say to yourself to keep going.

DONE IS BETTER THAN PERFECT

Time is the resource that can't be renewed or replaced

MY POWER STARTS WITH BEING RADICALLY HONEST WITH MYSELF

There is strength in asking for help

I HAVE THE RIGHT TO SAY NO

I give myself permission to try, and try again

Good enough *is enough*

I EMBRACE EVERY ASPECT OF MY HUMANNESS WITH SELF-COMPASSION

NO ONE KNOWS HOW TO LIVE MY LIFE BETTER THAN I DO

I am going to stay in my own lane and return to gratitude when I notice I've fallen into comparing

I am deserving and valuable and filling my own cup restores me so that I can give to others

I take responsibility for my feelings and actions and I give myself permission to go step by step in my own time

I can choose how I respond to my thoughts

I AM DESERVING OF THE EFFORT TO SCHEDULE MY TIME ACCORDING TO MY VALUES

I *acknowledge* where I went wrong, I *commit* to repairing what I can repair, and I *release* myself to take the wisdom I've learned and move forward towards my potential

My power lies in taking *action*

FLEXIBILITY ALLOWS ME TO MOVE FORWARD

I can have discomfort and take action

I may not be able to control what I feel, but I can control what I do

I can start where I am, with what I have